CREMATION, EMBALMMENT, OR NEITHER?

A Biblical/Christian Evaluation

ALVIN J. SCHMIDT

WESTBOW®
PRESS
A DIVISION OF THOMAS NELSON
& ZONDERVAN

WestBow Press books may be ordered through booksellers or by contacting:

WestBow Press
A Division of Thomas Nelson & Zondervan
1663 Liberty Drive
Bloomington, IN 47403
www.westbowpress.com
1 (866) 928-1240

ISBN: 978-1-4908-7209-4 (sc)
ISBN: 978-1-4908-7211-7 (hc)
ISBN: 978-1-4908-7210-0 (e)

Library of Congress Control Number: 2015903532

Print information available on the last page.

WestBow Press rev. date: 03/24/2015

CONTENTS

To my two sons, Timothy John and Mark Alvin

FOREWORD

In a day in which Christian authors are enthusiastically exploring such cutting edge topics as what the Bible teaches about exercise, weight loss and on-line dating, along comes a book whose mere title is a statement of cultural rebellion. Not many stir the embers of the fire, plunked down in their favorite overstuffed armchair, and settle into a cozy evening of reflecting on the subject of cremation and embalmment and the historical, cultural, and biblical reasons for Christian burial practices. Rarer still is that the author of this work hails from secular academia, and thus is academically and theologically qualified to do the scholarly research required to create the definitive treatment of the subject for our day. Such is the volume you now have in your hand.

Alvin Schmidt has never been known to shy away from controversial subjects. His earlier works have addressed a variety of objections raised to Christianity's truth claims (his prescient expose of Islam is a classic), including his extraordinary research on how Christianity has acted as a catalyst for progress in medicine, education, science, music, art and human rights over the past two millennia (*How Christianity Changed the World*). Now he has engaged his fertile cerebellum in another example of the way Christianity turned the world upside down in how it treated the human body, and in particular the treatment of that body after death.

John the Evangelist tells us that in the beginning was the Word and that Word was made manifest in the flesh, and indeed ever lives to intercede for fallen mankind as fully God and yet fully man, whose still evident wounds in His very flesh are now gazed upon by His ransomed followers. God made matter from the beginning and from Genesis to Revelation, flesh and blood are central to the biblical picture. Therefore Christians are to take special care how the dead are treated because they confess with the Church Ancient that there will be a resurrection of the bodies of all the dead in the final Eschaton. The Church Ancient was thus convinced that the dead are to be *buried* as a final witness to what the Church has always confessed about a general resurrection *of the body*.

What may come as a surprise to many (at least it was to me) was how counter-cultural the early Christians were in handling issues relating to the beginning and end of life and especially in its treatment of the dead human body. Rather than assimilate the pagan Roman practice of cremating the "useless remains," the earliest followers of Christ boldly buried their dead in reliance on the promise of the future resurrection of that same body explicitly taught by their Lord. Readers will learn, among a host of other fascinating facts, that the first case of a Christian being cremated with the sanction of the Church did not occur until the advent of the Enlightenment. Christian burial of the body (like infant baptism) was simply the norm of Christian experience and was the consistent practice and teaching of the Christian Church from the first century to the nineteenth.

Dr. Schmidt traces the centrality and sanctity of the matter in Christian theology and its impact on burial practices and in the process answers a question that has increasingly troubled me: Why is it so often the case that there is now no body present at Christian funerals anymore? The culprit once again is not the persuasive arguments of the non-Christian world but the spinelessness of the modern Christian Church in allowing culture to inform it of its practice rather than to first ask if our treatment of the body of those who have died is consistent with the teachings of the Incarnate Word.

This work is not only an apologetic for bringing the body back into funerals, but stands as a kind of Last Judgment on the contemporary acceptance in Christian circles of practices that are not only pagan in origin but in practice operate *contra* the Christian creedal confessions and consistent historical practice of the Church for almost two millennia. That confession and practice changed the entire climate of cultural opinion of the Roman world in three short centuries and was maintained inviolate until the rise of the Enlightenment and its romanticizing of ancient cultures, particularly Greece and its Platonic ideas about the centrality of the "spirit" and the relative unimportance of the material.

In a day and age where an objection to Christianity continues to be its supposed denigration of the fleshly and material world and other-worldly detachment from all things physical, Alvin Schmidt shows how grounded in gritty matter the biblical understanding of the world is and how we deny that physicality in our acceptance of gnostic, pagan and eastern philosophically based practices when it comes to dealing with death and its consequences.

This book is a clarion call to Christians to be consistent in practice with their confession when it comes to how they approach the final resting place of believers this side of the general resurrection of the dead. Dr. Schmidt has amassed historical, theological, biblical and practical evidences that the modern Christian church will only refuse to hear to its great loss both now and at the Judgment Seat of Christ where we each shall receive what is due us for things done "while in (might we also add "to") the body" (II Corinthians 5:10).

On the Feast of the Resurrection of Jesus 2015
Craig A. Parton, M.A., J.D.
Santa Barbara, California
United States Director, International Academy of Apologetics
(www.apologeticsacademy.eu)

PREFACE

Thirty years ago, it would not have occurred to me that I would research and publish a book dealing with cremation and embalmment. For one, very few people, especially Christians, then chose to have themselves cremated when their time came to leave this fallen world. But during the last three decades more and more people, including many Christians, have been opting for cremation. It is the latter that made me, a biblically minded Christian, sit up and think, so to speak, and ask: Is cremating human beings God-pleasing or not?

Second, I remembered my past reading and studying about the early Christians in Rome (stalwart followers of Christ) and their rejecting cremation, a common pagan practice. But I knew very little why they took that stance, for church historians have largely failed to address this important question. This is rather interesting given that Christianity's rejection of cremation resulted in the pagan Romans ending cremation by about the mid-300s. But even more important is the fact that the rejection of cremation became Christianity's the first culturally institutionalized norm in the West, and for almost two millennia earth burial was the only acceptable way to dispose of deceased human beings.

Third, during the last couple of decades, I have learned that most Christians are largely uninformed concerning Christianity's historical and theological reasons for rejecting cremation. Thus, I felt obligated to research this important matter, biblically, historically, and theologically and then share my findings with fellow Christians, many of whom I know are seriously asking and wondering whether it is God-pleasing or not to have themselves cremated. The pages that follow address this important Christian concern.

Fourth, during the past two decades in speaking to Christian groups in formal settings and interacting with them informally concerning the topic of cremation, I have frequently had Christians ask whether or not a Christian may, biblically speaking, have his or her deceased body embalmed. Thus, this book has an entire chapter devoted to embalmment, a common, cultural custom today, both in the United States and Canada when cremation is not chosen. That chapter examines and discusses embalmment historically, biblically, and theologically as it addresses the concern whether it is biblically correct or not for Christians to have their deceased bodies embalmed.

Finally, given that approximately 41 percent of deceased Americans today (2015) are cremated, and most others are embalmed, I am obviously swimming against the cultural stream by contending that cremation and embalmment both lack biblical and Christian theological support. To take this stance did not make it easy to write this book. It is never easy to question society's culturally taken-for-granted practices. Be that as it may, as a Christian, I sincerely hope and pray that this book not only will inform but also edify every devout Christian reader.

Soli Deo Gloria!

ACKNOWLEDGEMENTS

In my previously published books I expressed gratitude and appreciation to my wife Carol for patience and helpfulness, and I would be remiss if I did not do so again. She patiently tolerated my spending hours and days "holed up" in my study trying to create another book. As a sociologist, I am also conscious of the social isolation that writing a book requires. And again, my wife endured it all. So, Carol, many kind thanks!

I also want to thank the library staff at Illinois College, Jacksonville, Illinois, for obtaining inter-library books for my research. In a similar vein, the library at Concordia Seminary, St. Louis, Missouri, was exceedingly helpful in obtaining various inter-library materials. Washington University, St. Louis, Missouri, was also helpful as some of the staff assisted me in finding certain documents that greatly aided my research.

Last, but not least, I wish to express my appreciation to the staff at Westbow Press. Each member of the staff was both kind, helpful, and professional in responding to my editorial questions.

INTRODUCTION

This book, titled *Cremation, Embalmment, or Neither? A Biblical/ Christian Evaluation* is an expansion and revision of an earlier edition titled *Dust to Dust or Ashes to Ashes: A Biblical and Christian Examination of Cremation* (Salisbury, MA: Regina Orthodox Press, Inc., 2005). In addition to revising, updating, and expanding the chapters from the previous book, the present book has six new chapters. They are chapters 5, 7, 8, 11, 12, and 13.

Given that Christians from their earliest years in Rome opposed and rejected cremation and continued to do so throughout the Western world for nearly two thousand years, the first ten chapters of the book are primarily devoted to the topic of cremation. In regard to embalming the dead, the book devotes less space, the reason being that Christians in Rome and later in European countries buried their dead without embalming them. It was not until the late 1800s that Christians in the United States and Canada, for instance, began to embalm their dead. The practice never really appealed to Europeans.

As countries in Europe became Christianized, they abandoned cremation, and earth burial without embalmment became the cultural norm. Regarding embalmment, some exceptions did occasionally occur, for example, when certain individuals, Christian emperors or kings and some noteworthy monks, were sometimes embalmed (really mummified). Nonembalmmed burials are briefly discussed in chapter 12. In fact, it was not until the latter part of the 1800s that some Christians, especially in the United States and Canada, began to accept embalming, even though some churches initially did not support it. "To a mostly Christian population, embalming represented a pagan Egyptian practice that involved grotesque mutilation of the body, a kind of desecration of the human temple of God that was condemned in the New Testament."[1] The latter part of this citation reflects St. Paul's words written to the early Christians in Corinth. "Do you not know that you are God's temple and that God's Spirit dwells in you?" (I Corinthians 3:16).

There are hundreds of books published on the history of the Christian church that examine and discuss various aspects of the life and behavior of the early Christians. One phenomenon often discussed is the persecutions they experienced under the Romans during Christianity's first three hundred years. These books also discuss Christianity's church polity, its doctrinal conflicts, its geographic expansion, and how it became the West's predominant religion. But oddly enough, there is virtually a total absence of any discussion concerning early Christianity's consistent opposition and rejection of Rome's cremating of the dead. Most church history books even fail to make even a passing reference to cremation, and when cremation is noted, it consists of a mere sentence or two. This is quite astounding, for the Christian rejection of cremation was a major affront to the pagan Romans, an affront that sometimes resulted in Christians being persecuted, as is documented in chapter 6.

The Christian rejection of cremation was not an ephemeral phenomenon. Even after Christianity in AD 313 had received legal status with the Edict of Milan, Christians continued to spurn cremation for nearly two millennia. Thus, when various regions in Europe became Christianized and pagans converted to Christianity, they "were required to give up cremation in favor of the Christian custom of earth burial."[2]

There is a paucity of information in church history books regarding Christianity's spurning cremation, and they also fail to note that by the eleventh century earth burial had become the only acceptable way to dispose of dead humans in all Europe. And it is further astounding because the Christian rejection of cremation became the first institutionalized cultural change Christianity accomplished in the Western world. In addition to this major cultural change, the present book also examines and discusses the biblical and theological reasons that prompted early Christians and their descendants in the West to reject Rome's cremation. Interestingly, from the fourth century, when the pagan Romans had stopped cremating their dead, there was no longer any formal opposition to Christianity's rejection of cremation in the West until the mid-nineteenth century.

In addition to the historical background regarding Christianity's rejection of cremation, this book also provides information intended to provide today's Christians with some theological insights about why their spiritual ancestors from the earliest days of the church, and for centuries after, continued to reject cremation until the latter half of the twentieth century. It was then that virtually all Christian denominations, contrary to Christians of the past, no longer opposed or rejected cremation but even accepted it.

It is well-known today that most Christian clergy and theologians "in tune" with their respective denominations have largely acquiesced to the practice of cremation. Thus, today's Christians receive little or no guidance from their pastors or priests about whether cremation is biblically acceptable. Countless clergy tell their members that the Bible does not forbid cremation. Hence, members are left to conclude that choosing to be buried or cremated is a personal decision, devoid of any biblical, theological guidance. In contacting leaders and officials in mainline denominations, I have found the void of biblical guidance is common and widespread. Moreover, the early Christians who rejected cremation are not presented to today's Christians as role models. Thus, numerous Christians today know little or nothing about the historical fact that their spiritual ancestors in the Roman era and later consistently spurned cremation.

The book's first chapter surveys and discusses the rising rates of cremation since the mid-1960s in the Western world. This chapter notes various factors that have prompted and continue to prompt the rising rates, one being theological quiescence on the part of churches. An instance of theological quiescence occurred in 1710 in Ireland when the first known cremation in Europe took place by a church member, Mrs. John Pratt, who had herself cremated (discussed in chapter 7). The churches were silent. Another factor contributing to the rising rates was the formal acceptance of cremation by the Roman Catholic Church that occurred in 1963, an acceptance that other Christian denominations soon imitated.

Chapter 2 discusses the pagan roots and origins of cremation. It also cites some of the reasons why people of different religions or cultures (Hindus, ancient Greeks, Romans, and some American Indians) chose to incinerate their dead.

The third chapter, "Hebrews Rejected Cremation," focuses on why the Hebrews in the Old Testament, in contrast to their pagan neighbors, rejected burning their dead. This chapter also takes a close look at various biblical passages and how some have either been ignored or misrepresented by cremationists.

Chapter 4, "Cremation: Past and Present," looks at how cremation was practiced in the past and how it differs from today's cremation process. The chapter also notes some aspects not commonly known, namely that the cremated remains (commonly called *ashes*) consist not just of ashes but also contain the unburned bones that are now pulverized (ground up) in every cremation. Thus, the funeral industry prefers to call this mixture *cremains*, but this new word has not been accepted by the general public, for it keeps calling the cremated remains ashes. Given that most articles and books use the term ashes when cremated remains are discussed, I have retained the word ashes in the following pages. This present chapter also cites data showing that today's cremation process is a major source of air pollution.

The fifth chapter, "From Cremating to Composting," discusses two new methods of disposing human bodies promoted by concerned environmentalists. One method is known as *resomation*, a process that breaks down the body chemically (dissolves it) by submerging it in a tubular-steel chamber filled with a liquid solution of alkaline hydrolysis. This process finally yields a white flour–like powder that may be scattered or placed into an urn. The second method is known as *promession*. This method was invented in Sweden in 1999. It freezes the deceased body at eighteen degrees Celsius (four degrees Fahrenheit) for about ten days and then submerges the body in liquid nitrogen that makes it brittle. Then it is pulverized by a vibrating method. The final product is a dry powder that may be used as compost material.

The sixth chapter is titled "The Early Christians Rejected Cremation." It begins by noting that the early Christians saw themselves as resident aliens (*paroikoi*), vis-à-vis the pagan Romans. It was an important self-concept that helped them remain united in the face of pagan hatred, in part because they rejected cremation. This chapter also discusses various reasons that motivated Christians to reject cremation, and it shows that their persistent rejection of cremation—oddly enough—was not the result of any formally mandated canon of a church synod or council.

Chapter 7 discusses how the return of cremation in the West in the mid-1800s became problematic for biblically minded Christians. For one, it contradicts the theological meaning of the English word *cemetery*; second, it ignores cremation's destructively violent process; third, it misuses the word ashes; fourth, in the minds of many it casts doubt on the Christian doctrine of the body's future resurrection; fifth, it gives spiritual offense to many Christians and non-Christians; sixth, it contradicts many Christian hymns that speak of the dead lying in their graves; and seventh, it fails to recognize the oxymoronic term of so-called "cremation cemeteries."

"Christianity's Burial Symbolism" is the title of the eighth chapter. It discusses the role symbolism plays in Christians having retained their centuries-old practice of earth burial. These symbols include death as "sleep;" calling graveyards *koimeteria* in Greek or *coemeteria* in Latin (both meant sleeping places); bringing the dead into the city; conducting funerals in churches; seeing death as the day of birth (*dies natalis*); and Christians commonly using the east–west axis for their graves.

Chapter 9 discusses the churches' capitulation to cremation in terms of their ignoring how and why their spiritual ancestors, the early Christians, for nearly two millennia had unequivocally opposed and rejected cremation. This chapter also notes some of the factors that led churches to accept cremation.

The book's tenth chapter, "Cremation Miscellanea," discusses various matters related to cremation. They reveal the direct correlation between secularism and cremation; whether the churches' acceptance of cremation has weakened their gospel message; the argument that says land is for the living, not for burying the dead; cremation as a cultural revolution; the acceptance of cremation that desensitized people to its destructive nature; inhumation and expensive funerals; memorial services and their relationship to cremation; funerals and clergy redundancy; catastrophic fires vis-à-vis cremation; funeral directors and funeral homes; a death-denial culture; and Christian counsel for Christians who have been a party to a cremation.

Chapter 11 is titled "Churches Acquiesced to Funeral Directors." It documents and discusses the growth and influence funeral directors have had in the United States and Canada and how Christians and their pastors have uncritically accepted funeral practices that often are in conflict with Christian theological beliefs and values.

Chapter 12 focuses on the embalming practice and is titled, "Embalming: Is It Biblically Correct?" It indicates that embalmment, similar to cremation, was not practiced by the early Christians in Rome. Apart from the exception of some early, deviant Christians in Egypt, Christians from their earliest years consistently buried their dead without embalming them. This chapter also notes how the practice of embalming by Christians has since the late 1800s become a culturally institutionalized custom. This is especially true in the United States and Canada, largely because it has not been critically or biblically evaluated, despite embalmment's physical assault on the human corpse, together with the highly toxic, hazardous fluids that are injected into the body and then transferred to the soil via the buried body.

The thirteenth chapter, the conclusion chapter, enumerates what Christians are not taught or told by the churches' teachers, clergy, and theologians with regard to the early Christians who opposed and rejected Rome's pagan practice of cremation. Nor are Christians informed that the Christian rejection of cremation in part contributed to the pagan Romans abandoning cremation in the fourth century. And they are also not informed of why their early ancestors continued to reject cremation and practiced only earth burial for nearly two thousand years. This final chapter also notes what Christians are not taught or told about embalming (an old pagan practice), and the various problems it presents for concerned Christians today.

Biblical quotations are from the English Standard Version (ESV), unless otherwise noted.

---

1   Martin Harris, *Grave Matters: A Journey Through The Modern Funeral Industry To A Natural Way Of Burial* (New York: Scribner, 2007), 45.

2   John F. McDonald, "Cremation," *The Jurist* (1966), 230.

CHAPTER 1

RISING RATES OF CREMATION

Whenever you find yourself on the side of the
majority, it is time to pause and reflect.
—Mark Twain

It can be argued that it was largely the result of Christianity's influence that cremation, once a prevalent practice among the pagan Romans, ended in the empire in the fourth century.[1] Before the Romans stopped cremating their dead, the early Christians had consistently opposed and rejected cremation, and they did so without any formally mandated prohibition. It was not until Charlemagne the Great that Christianity's informal opposition was legally reinforced when he made cremation a capital crime in the Holy Roman Empire in AD 785.[2] However, even after Charlemagne had outlawed cremation, it still lingered on for a couple of centuries in some regions in northern Europe, like Scandinavia and Britain. But when Denmark, for instance, became Christianized, burning the dead ceased in its regions in about 1000.[3] The situation was similar in Sweden, where cremation ended in 1050, after it too had become Christianized.[4] Similarly, Britain abandoned cremation in the eleventh century, again as the result of Christianization.[5]

Then, for almost a thousand years after, earth burial was the only method for the disposition of the dead in all of Europe. Although not legally required, earth burial also became the exclusive practice in the Americas and in Australasia. Thus, residents of the New World, as in Europe, disposed of their dead only by inhumation, and it was not until the latter half of the 1800s that cremation was brought back from the pagan era of ancient Rome. However, upon its reappearance in the last quarter of the nineteenth century, it received only minimal acceptance for a number of decades. Most Westerners, still strongly influenced by Christianity's longstanding rejection of cremation, saw it as unthinkable or even "bizarre."[6] For instance, in 1900, there were only 2,414 (.003 percent) deceased persons cremated in the entire United States, and sixty years later, the American cremation rate was still quite low, with 60,987 (3.56 percent) of the deceased cremated. But in the 1960s, a decade that historians call "the radical '60s," many traditional cultural norms were challenged and even rejected. Promoting cremation in place of earth burial is one example.

Thus, in the 1960s, cremation rates began to increase and spiral upwardly in the succeeding five decades. By the year 2010, the number of cremations in the United States, for example, had risen to 40.62 percent of deceased Americans. In Canada, which had essentially the same rate as the United States in 1960, the rate had increased even more rapidly. Hence, by 2010, the Canadian rate had climbed to 58.17 percent, and in some provinces the rate was higher still.[7]

When one looks at European countries, it is noteworthy that France, a highly secular society that Voltaire once described as having more "baptized pagans than any other country," had a relatively low rate of 13 percent in the late 1990s, but by 2010 it had tripled to 30 percent. Italy, on the other hand, still had a relatively low rate of 13 percent in 2010, while Ireland's figure in the same year was lower still at 11 percent, and in Poland the rate in 2010 stood at 9 percent.[8]

These latter three countries are still outside the current upward trend, whereas the United Kingdom in 2010 had 74 percent of its deceased humans cremated. In the Czech Republic, for instance, the rate in 2010 stood at 80 percent; 85 percent in Switzerland; 77 percent in Denmark[9]; and 47 percent in Germany.[10]

The rise in cremation rates has of course resulted in a corresponding rise in crematories. The United States in 1960, for example, had 232 crematories, but in 2010 it had 2,113.[11] In some countries, the rising rates of cremation are becoming problematic. Switzerland's residents, for instance, have recently complained that Lake Constance is becoming the "Lake of the Dead," given that numerous Germans from the north are tossing cremated remains into the lake.

Turning to Greece, we find the cremation rate is essentially zero because the Greek Orthodox Church is strongly opposed to cremation. Until recently, it was even able to persuade the nation's parliament to outlaw cremation for those who are not members of the Greek Orthodox Church. The Greek church's opposition to cremation, according to the *Athens News* (September 24, 2012), is based on theological grounds that sees the human body "as the temple of the Holy Spirit," and thus not to be destroyed by fire, even after the "temple" dies. According to the *Athens News*, if a member of the Greek Orthodox Church desires cremation, he or she has to have it done in another European country. Hence, in recent years, approximately a thousand Greeks have had themselves cremated elsewhere, usually in Bulgaria. But in 2006, the church agreed to the country's parliament legalizing cremation for nonchurch members and also for foreigners. In addition, it agreed to support a legislative bill that allowed a crematory to be built in 2012 in Zografou, a municipality of Athens. However, given the Greek church's long-standing opposition to cremation, analysts say this crematory will be the only one in Greece for a long time to come.

As history shows, "The early Christians, following the example of the Jews, abhorred cremation."[12] Thus, by continuing to reject cremation, Greece, unlike other Western countries that have accepted it, stands closest to the early Christians.

Why the Acceleration?

After the Christianization of European countries had largely been achieved by the twelfth century, earth burial had become the only acceptable way to dispose of dead humans in the West. It had become taken for granted. But early in the eighteenth century, the first rejection of earth burial occurred when a Mrs. John Pratt, wife of Ireland's treasurer, had herself cremated in 1710. Sometime after her cremation, an inscribed stone was found that called her a "worthy woman" for having chosen cremation.[13]

The Enlightenment

From the mid-seventeenth century through the eighteenth century, a new intellectual movement, the Enlightenment or Age of Reason, arose in the West. Its proponents argued that knowledge and meaning in life were to be acquired from the use of human reason, rather than from tradition and biblical authority. They rejected biblical revelation and the miracles recorded in the Bible. This resulted in questioning and often rejecting many of Christianity's long-standing teachings and practices.

To what degree Mrs. Pratt was influenced by the Enlightenment is not known, but her questioning Christianity's centuries-old practice of earth burial by her opting for cremation was highly compatible with this new philosophy. Similarly, it is not an exaggeration to say the rise of the cremation movement in the 1800s was also compatible with Enlightenment thinking. However, after the movement had become established, by 1874 very few Westerners for the next seventy to eighty years chose to be cremated. But by the 1960s, the Enlightenment's philosophy of rejecting traditional Christian practices had apparently changed the minds of an increasing number of Westerners, including many Christians, as more and more turned from earth burial to cremation. It seems apparent that Christians who since the mid-1960s have opted for cremation do not realize they are accepting the value of a philosophy that is foreign to historic, biblical Christianity. Nor do they realize that they have distanced themselves from their spiritual ancestors, the early Christians, who valiantly rejected cremation and often experienced persecution for insisting on being buried rather than cremated.

Sounds of Silence from the Churches

Another variable that sheds light on why cremation rates have risen so rapidly since the 1960s and are continuing to rise in part goes back to the churches—both Catholic and Protestant—for having failed to renounce Mrs. Pratt's cremation in 1710. No record exists showing that churches even took note of her deviant act. Why they were silent is unknown. Perhaps they saw her cremation as an isolated event, one that would likely not happen again.

By remaining silent in the Pratt case, the churches failed to show Christians in Ireland and elsewhere that cremation contradicted the biblical principles that the Hebrews adhered to in the Old Testament and Christianity's rejection of cremation from its earliest years in Rome. By their silence, the churches also failed to note why Christians for centuries, from their earliest years in Rome, had rejected cremation.

In the early 1800s, the churches again were taciturn when pro-cremationists actively began to promote their cause as some even performed cremations in different parts of Europe. The following are some examples. In 1815, four thousand fallen soldiers were burned after the Battle of Waterloo.[14] Soon another cremation took place when Percy Bysshe Shelley, the British poet, was cremated on a beach in 1822 after he drowned while residing in Italy. He was an atheist and the husband of Mary Wollstonecraft Shelley, author of *Frankenstein* (1818).[15] In 1855, Johann Peter Trusen, a regimental physician in the Prussian army, published a pro-cremation book,

Die Leichenverbrennung als das Geeignetste art der Todtenbestattung (*Cremation as the Preferred Way to Dispose of the Dead*). Following Trusen's book, a number of additional efforts unfolded promoting cremation. In 1857, Ferdinando Coletti, a scientist and university professor, advocated cremation at a conference in Italy. Ten years later (1867), cholera victims were cremated at Pergamino, Buenos Aires, Argentina. In 1870, the Prussian army used portable cremators during the Franco-Prussian War (1870–71). Meanwhile, in 1872, three professors conducted cremation experiments in Italy, and the same year poorly buried corpses of soldiers who were killed in the Battle of Sedan (1870) were cremated.[16] But no records seem to exist showing ecclesiastical objections.

The silence of the churches regarding Mrs. Pratt's cremation in 1710 and the silence pertaining to other cremation events that occurred intermittently (as just cited) in the first half of the 1800s enabled the movement to establish a firm foothold by the latter part of the 1800s. This foothold, to a large degree, was the result of two men, Lodovico Brunetti and Sir Henry Thompson. Brunetti, professor at Italy's Padua University, demonstrated at the Vienna Exposition in 1873 that a human corpse could be burned by using a gas or coal furnace instead of a pyre of wood. Thompson, a British physician from England, was greatly impressed upon seeing Brunetti's furnace with its incinerated results. Returning to England from Vienna, he published a pro-cremation article in *The Contemporary Review* (January, 1874). The article was highly critical of earth burial. The same year Thompson also founded The Cremation Society of England.

As was true of many cremationists at that this time, Thompson was an agnostic. Aside from his pro-cremation views and activities, he was known as a polymath and Queen Victoria's physician. Whether his being the queen's physician enhanced his social status and hence aided his pro-cremation objectives is not certain. Although Thompson had successfully introduced cremation in England in 1874 by founding The Cremation Society of England, it is noteworthy that the success of the movement was not confined to England, for in 1874 the New York Cremation Society also came into existence. And the same year cremation societies were also formed in Switzerland, Austria, and the Netherlands.[17] Cremation in the West had come back from ancient Rome to stay.

The Papacy Breaks the Silence

The Vicariate Apostolic of Vizagapatatum of the Roman Catholic Church in India in September 1884 responded to a question two parents had asked about the status of two neophyte Christians who had been cremated. In part, the response said, "You must not approve of cremation."[18] This statement, however, was not directed at the cremation movement that had established itself in England and the United States ten years earlier.

The Holy See's first formal response regarding the cremation movement and its activities came when Pope Leo XIII in 1886 issued two anticremation decrees, one in September and the other in December. The September decree condemned cremation and barred Christians from belonging to a cremation society, and it declared "the unlawfulness of demanding cremation for one's own body or that of another."[19] The decree in December mostly reinforced what had been issued in September.

Then in 1892, the Holy See issued a third decree; it asserted that Catholics were not to cooperate in any act of cremation.[20] It also stated, "Anyone who has requested that his body shall be cremated shall be deprived of ecclesiastical burial unless he has shown signs of repentance before death" (*Corpus Juris Canonici*, ca. 1240).[21] Then, in 1917, the Code of Canon Law "prohibited ecclesiastical burial of bodies that were to be cremated."[22] This action was followed by another decree, this one from Pope Pius XI in 1926. It again condemned cremation, saying its promoters were "enemies of

Christianity." The decree also warned that cremation de-emphasized the resurrection of the body.[23]

However, these decrees mostly spoke of punishing those who chose cremation. They could have cited some reasons why the early Christians, for instance, had firmly maintained their rejection of cremation among the pagan Romans from the latter half of the first century. But they said nothing about Christianity's history of rejecting cremation. And Protestant denominations at this time in the late 1800s said nothing at all about cremation. They seemed to ignore it.

The Holy See's renunciations also failed to mention that cremating the dead was abandoned in European countries and regions when they became Christianized in the Middle Ages. As one observer noted, "Burial of the dead had become so much a part of the Christian heritage that when the barbarian peoples were converted to Christianity they were required to give up the practice of cremation in favor of the Christian custom burial."[24] Thus, Christians regarded church membership and earth burial as inseparable, or two sides of the same coin. But by the early 1700s, even though Christians continued to practice only earth burial, it appears they no longer knew that their spiritual ancestors, back to the latter part of the first century, had consistently rejected cremation when they lived among the pagan Romans, and that their rejection had continued for centuries after. And it also appears Christians at this time did not know the early Christians had theological reasons for practicing earth burial. Now, they evidently buried their dead because it had always been done that way. Earth burial had simply become a taken-for-granted practice.

Although the Holy See broke the silence regarding cremation, its decrees seemed to have had little or no effect. For its edicts really failed to address and inform Christians why their spiritual ancestors in the preceding centuries, from their time in Rome, had stalwartly opposed and rejected cremation.

Major Theological and Historical Omissions

It is noteworthy that the early church had no written rule or ecclesiastical canon barring members from cremating their dead. Neither did it have a formally stated position delineating the theological reasons for rejecting cremation, even though a few church fathers (e.g., Tertullian, late second and early third century, and Lactantius, early fourth century) cited some reasons of their own for not cremating the dead. Nevertheless, the early Christians continued unequivocally to reject cremation, not just at the time of the pagan Romans but until the early eighteenth century when the first known deviation occurred by Mrs. Pratt in Ireland in 1710. Looking back, one not only finds no ecclesiastical condemnation of her cremation but also no statement revealing biblically based reasons that motivated the early Christians in their rejection of cremation in preceding centuries. The absence of such a statement(s) may rightly be seen as a major theological omission—a real lacuna—that existed at least from 1710 to the mid-1800s.

Given this existing lacuna, it is not surprising that only thirty-seven years after the Holy See's last renunciation of cremation in 1926, Pope Paul VI in 1963 issued *De Cadaverum Crematione* (Concerning the Cremation of the Dead). This document ignored and even contradicted arguments of the Vatican's previous renunciations because now Roman Catholics were permitted to have themselves cremated, providing it was not done for reasons hostile to Christianity. Pope Paul VI had turned the Catholic church 180 degrees from its previous anticremation statements, and in so doing, he also ignored virtually two thousand years of Christian opposition to cremation. In short, the Roman Catholic Church, via the papal office, had succumbed to the secular culture without admitting it. Acquiescing to cremation in 1963 also contradicted some of the church's previous excommunications of members who had supported cremation. For instance, during World War II the

Catholic church excommunicated several Germans for having taken a pro-cremation stance.[25]

In addition to the Roman Catholic Church having made an about-face in 1963, it is noteworthy that the Church of England officially followed suit in 1969 by formally giving the green light to its members concerning cremation, although it had already been accepting cremated remains in Westminster Abbey since 1910, especially those of high-status individuals.[26] In the United States the Episcopal church, the counterpart of the Church of England, had already taken a pro-cremation stance in 1896 when it built the first crematory in Milwaukee, Wisconsin.[27]

When the pope on behalf of the Roman Catholic Church formally condoned cremation in 1963, he did not do it (as noted earlier) on the basis of a theological study of the problem. Influenced by secular culture, he merely issued a statement condoning it. Similarly, most other Christian denominations (with the exception of the Eastern Orthodox churches), since cremation's return to the West in the late 1800s, have gone along with the practice by also having never issued any theological defense of Christianity's centuries-old rejection of cremation. Similar to the Catholic church, they acquiesced to the secular culture. Hence, the comment by the British theologian J. Douglas Davies (a cremationist) is noteworthy. He said, "Most churches have become deeply involved in it [cremation], but they have paid relatively little formal attention to theological issues involved."[28]

Given the absence of theologically based critiques regarding cremation, Christians were unprepared to defend earth burial when the cremation movement appeared in the nineteenth century. It is doubtful whether Christians even knew that their spiritual forebearers from the earliest years of the church's existence had despised and spurned cremation. If some knew, it is still not likely that they really knew and understood *why* the early Christians had taken that stance. And it is also not likely that they knew the Christian opposition to the Roman practice of cremation often came at a high price because for many it brought ridicule, hatred, and sometimes physical persecution in the early years of their presence in Rome.

After cremation among the Romans came to an end in the fourth century, Christians no longer faced the cultural pressure to conform to the pagan way of disposing of the dead. Thus, for fifteen hundred years, they were free to bury their dead as God's people did in the Old and New Testament era. They undoubtedly rejoiced when they saw converts from paganism abandon cremation as countries and regions in which they resided became Christianized. Earth burial had become an institutionalized practice, even though the church had never formally prohibited parishioners from burning their dead, and throughout the Middle Ages they also had never issued a known, formal theological position regarding inhumation versus cremation with insights drawn from the early church's experience. With no one deviating from the custom of burying the dead, they apparently saw no need for a formal, theological position. Moreover, they evidently did not envision a time when centuries of earth burial would be challenged and rejected by some in the church in favor of the pagan custom of incinerating the dead.

In trying to understand why there has been the remarkable rise in cremation rates since the 1960s history seems to point to the lack of theological conviction, even negligence, on the part of many clergy and theologians. It is they who failed to inform and educate church members in regard to why God's people saw cremation in the Old and New Testament as not pleasing to God. And given that no Christian denomination has ever produced a biblically based study in defense of Christianity's longstanding practice of earth burial vis-à-vis cremation, numerous church members in most denominations now follow in ignorance what their culture in recent years has defined as acceptable. This situation prompts an important question. If the early Christians, resting in their graves, knew that many of today's Christians—their spiritual descendants—are now choosing cremation, would they, to use an old phrase, turn over in their graves?

The Social Desire to Conform

Along with the churches' clergy and theologians not having informed their members why Christians for centuries shunned cremation, and thus unwittingly contributed to the rise in cremation rates, there is still another factor why many Christians are now opting for cremation. It is the human desire to conform to society's cultural beliefs and practices. This is a desire most individuals usually do not consciously recognize. But as sociological research shows, conforming socially and culturally makes people feel accepted; it gives them a sense of belonging. Hence, as cremation is increasingly becoming an acceptable way for the disposition of the dead, more and more individuals, including many Christians, are conforming to this secular practice. They seem to be unaware of St. Paul's admonition to the Christians in Rome not to conform to this world (Romans 12:2).

Some Individual Responses to Cremation

As cremation rates began to rise in the 1960s, Christianity's historical and biblical reasons for retaining inhumation have received very little or no support from publications written by various individuals since then. The following are some examples. In 1965 James W. Fraser, for instance, published a small book titled *Cremation: Is It Christian?* Although his book contends that cremation is biblically wrong and un-Christian, it does not reveal or discuss Christianity's historical opposition to it. The book also overlooks the secular forces that prompted cremation's reappearance, and it devotes no attention to the clergy and churches that were beginning to tolerate or even condone it.

A second small book titled *Cremation* appeared in 1968. It was penned by Paul E. Irion, a professor of pastoral theology. His book provides a brief history of cremation and has a number of pages discussing Christian concerns regarding cremation. But as a whole, its author sees no problems with Christians choosing cremation.

A third publication worthy of note is a small volume, *Cremation: Today and Tomorrow* (1990), by J. Douglas Davies. It cites some theological anomalies inherent in cremation funeral services as conducted in many churches today. For instance, as he points out, "The rites they [the clergy] perform still assume underlying ideas derived from the traditional funeral service of burial."[29] Given that this assumption is basically incorrect, he composed a liturgy for clergy who perform cremation funerals. The liturgy appears at the end of his book.

A fourth volume, *Cremation Concerns* (1989), was written by William E. Phipps, an American professor of religion. In his advocating for cremation, he cites dubious biblical passages taken from contexts that do not pertain to cremation or even to the disposing of deceased bodies. In chapter 7, I evaluate some of his pro-cremation arguments.

A fifth book, *Purified by Fire: A History of Cremation in America* (2001), was authored by Stephen Prothero, a professor of religion. As its subtitle indicates, it is a historical survey of cremation in the United States. Although the book contains some references to cremation in terms of how it affects traditional Christian theology, that, however, is not its primary focus. For the most part, Prothero's book is a pro-cremation treatise. It reveals no sympathy for traditional Christianity's opposition to cremation.

These books, and others written in this manner, tend to encourage Christians to conclude that cremation is an acceptable option for them. Moreover, only a few published articles in the last several decades have appeared critical of cremation, and these have likely not come to the attention of many Christians.

Conclusion

The rapid rise in cremation rates since the 1960s indicates cremation has become a culturally imbedded practice increasingly preempting earth burial that once was a major Christian imprint on Western culture for virtually two millennia. People opting for cremation now are largely the product of secularization spawned by Enlightenment philosophy, along with Christian clergy and theologians having failed to inform and educate church members that there were biblical and theological reasons why Christians for nearly two millennia practiced only inhumation from the earliest days of their existence in pagan Rome.

Christians, at least by the early 1700s, seemed to have been uninformed, as first evidenced by the Pratt case, about why their spiritual predecessors for centuries had practiced earth burial. This information lacuna greatly aided secular-minded cremationists in achieving their objectives in the West by 1874. From the early 1700s cremationists seemed to have encountered no formal, ecclesiastical opposition, and when some opposition finally did appear in the late 1800s, it was too little and too late, for the cremationists had already attainted their objectives. And interestingly, church leaders still continued to keep Christians historically and theologically uninformed about why their spiritual ancestors for centuries had practiced only earth burial in opposition to cremation.

---

[1]   Some historians, however, think it is not correct to credit Christianity with the cessation of cremation in the fourth century. One of them is A. D. Nock. See his article, "Cremation and Burial in the Roman Empire," *Harvard Theological Review* (October, 1932), 326. On the other hand, an early member of The Cremation Society in England (founded in 1874), John Castleman Swinburne-Hanham, argued it was Christianity's influence that led to Rome's ending cremation. See his article "Cremation," *The Encyclopedia Britannica* (Cambridge, England: At the University Press, 1910), 7:403.

[2]   Some publications have stated that Constantine the Great, the emperor of the Roman Empire, outlawed cremation soon after Christianity had received

legal status in AD 313. But none of them provide any documentation. In my research I have not been able to verify this reputed action by Constantine.

3   Douglas J. Davies and Lewis H. Mates, *Encyclopedia of Cremation* (Burlington, VT: Ashgate Publishing Company, 2005), 162.

4   Ibid., 458.

5   Ibid.

6   William Flanagan, "The New (and More Convenient) American Way of Death," *Forbes* (October, 1996), 324.

7   National Funeral Directors Association (www.nfda.org/media-center/stasticsreports.html), accessed September 23, 2012.

8   "International Cremation Statistics, 2010," *Pharos International* (Winter, 2011), 33.

9   Ibid.

10   *Association Francaise d' Information Funeraire,* Paris, France.

11   "International Cremation Statistics, 2010," *Pharos International* (Winter, 2011), 37.

12   Sir Arnold Wilson and Herman Levy, *Burial Reform and Funeral Costs* (London: Oxford University Press, 1938), 5.

13   Florence G. Fidler, *Cremation* (London: Williams and Norgate, 1930), 18.

14   Davies and Mates, op. cit., 459.

15   Ibid.

16   Ibid., 460.

17   Ibid.

18   William Devlin, "Cremation," *The Catholic Encyclopedia* (New York: Robert Appleton Company, 1908), 4:482.

19   Ibid., 460.

20   Ibid.

21   R. Rutherford, "Cremation," *The New Catholic Encyclopedia* (Detroit: Thompson and Gale, 2003), 4:359.

22   Ibid.

23   M. B. Walsh, "Cremation (Moral Aspect)," *New Catholic Encyclopedia* (San Francisco: McGraw-Hill, 1967), 4:1.

24   John F. McDonald, "Cremation," *The Jurist* (1966), 206.

25   Anthony Adolph, anthonyadolph.co.uk/cremation-in-britain (accessed February 24, 2014)

26   William E. Phipps, *Cremation Concerns* (Springfield, IL: Charles C. Thomas Publisher, 1989), 58.

27   Ibid.

28   J. Douglas Davies, *Cremation Today and Tomorrow* (Bramcote, England: Grove Books Limited, 1990), 6.

29   Ibid.

CHAPTER 2

CREMATION'S PAGAN ROOTS

There is something pagan in me that I cannot shake off.
—Lord Byron

Derived from the Latin *cremare* (to burn), cremation is the process of destroying a deceased human body by fire. As might be surmised, it is not the oldest method of disposing a human corpse, for I know of no historian who in studying the history of how people have disposed of deceased human bodies has ever denied the words of John Jamieson. "As far as we can judge from historical records, the primeval mode of disposing of dead bodies was by inhumation."[1] In fact, historical evidence indicates that burning dead human beings apparently did not occur until about two thousand years before the birth of Christ.

Given that this chapter shows cremation has pagan roots, and that the term *pagan* is often used in the present book, I am providing a brief definition. The word *pagan* comes from the Latin word *pagani,* meaning rural dwellers as opposed to urbanites. Since early Christianity was largely an urban phenomenon, Christians, in contrast to others, used the term *pagani* (rural residents) for those who did not believe that Jesus was God's incarnate Son who was crucified and raised from the dead.

Robin Lane Fox also tells us pagans had religious rites, even though they had no formal creed and had no concept of heresy or orthodoxy.[2] Its adherents worshiped terrestrial and celestial things.[3] And sincerity was never an issue, for neither one's fellow worshipers nor one's gods cared about sincerity. Some outward ritualistic compliance was sufficient.[4] Paganism's multiple gods possessed all human frailties, but people still worshiped them to appease the deities' anger. Pagans made no exhortations to faith, and neither did they see themselves as the faithful ones.[5] Thus, they had no concept of faith as the Christians had. To Christians faith meant firmly believing in the effects or benefits of biblical event(s) that had empirically happened—for example, miracles and the physical resurrection of Jesus Christ, as Paul argued and vouched for in 1 Corinthians 15, where he states that he and the apostles, plus some five hundred people, had personally seen the bodily resurrected Jesus.

Some Ancient Reasons for Cremating the Dead

In surveying the subject of cremation, reasons why it was done are more easily found than is the exact time or place of its origin. Some scholars think the burning of human corpses began because ancient people feared the dead, so they thought destroying them by fire coped with that fear. Another reason—rather widely held—was that cremation enabled the survivors to carry the bones of the deceased, especially those of warriors, back to their homes or to some other desirable place.[6] Still another reason for incinerating human corpses is mentioned by the Roman writer Pliny the Elder (AD 23–79). He says the ancient Greeks practiced cremation in part to prevent buried bodies from being stolen by thieves or disturbed by other miscreants (*Natural History* 7:54).

In some instances, dead bodies were burned because people believed in the pagan notion that fire freed the soul from wandering and searching for rest after the person had expired. Related to this belief, some groups thought fire separated the human spirit from the body.[7] The latter belief is still held by many Hindus in India today.

However, the Hindus also cremate their dead because they believe fire spiritually purifies the deceased person's soul. Many of the two hundred songs and poems of the Upanishads (a Rig Veda collection of Hinduism's spiritual songs and teachings) speak about funeral fires purifying the soul.[8] Among the Todas in India the corpse was burned facedown because it was believed that such a position facilitated the soul's journey into the ground below.[9] The Pomo Indians in California also burned their dead facedown because they believed that allowed "the spirit to more easily lift itself to journey to the afterworld."[10] And the Tlingit Indians in southern Alaska burned their dead in a reclining position so that dead person's soul could "more easily arise and go forth."[11]

Still another reason for cremating the dead had to do with the belief that the soul at death entered another living creature. Thus, Kashaya Pomo Indians in California cremated their deceased "not only to protect the body from wild animals but also to prevent the body from becoming a wild animal itself ..."[12] And while the Cheyenne Indians did not believe the soul could enter a wild animal, they cremated those "guilty of murder, suicide, incest, or promiscuity [so that the ghost or soul would] vanish into oblivion."[13] There were, however, also many Indian tribes in the Americas that did not cremate their deceased members.

Time and Place of Cremation's Origin and Expansion

Among the Hindus, who use cremation virtually as the only method to dispose of their dead, cremation came into existence about 2000 BC,[14] and it is quite likely that India is also the place where cremating humans first originated. One scholar thinks, "Cremation was brought by barbarians from the East [India] to the Mediterranean basin about 2500–2000 BC, where previously the practice was unknown."[15] In ancient Greece it evidently appeared considerably later, about 1000 BC. But apparently it was well-established by the time of the Greek poet Homer (ca. ninth century BC). In the *Iliad* (book 23), Homer describes in detail the cremation of Patroclus, the fallen Greek warrior who fought the Trojans. Homer also provides considerable information in the *Iliad* (book 24) regarding the cremation of Hector, the leader of the Trojans. He does not, however, give the impression that cremation was the only method of disposing of the dead among the Greeks; nor could he, for some of the Greek poets (for instance, Sophocles cited below) still talked about earth burial long after Homer's time. And Plutarch (ca. AD 46–ca.120), in his *Parallel of Illustrious Greeks and Romans*, observes that among the Spartans inhumation prevailed (*Lycurgus* 27:1–2). This indicates earth burial was still common among many ancient Greeks in the eighth century BC.

That the ancient Greeks greatly valued earth burial without embalmment is clearly seen in Sophocles' *Antigone,* a fifth-century BC tragic drama. It shows Antigone, a Greek woman, challenging King Creon's edict that barred her from burying her dead brother Polyneices, who had been declared a political traitor. Antigone believed firmly that her brother, as a human being, traitor or not, should receive earth burial rather than leave him exposed to roaming dogs, wolves, or vultures. To deny him burial, she believed, was contrary to a higher (natural) law of the gods, and so she defied the king's order and buried him, an act that resulted in her being condemned to death by the king. The blind prophet Teiresias, in this drama, also believed in burial, for he warned the king that in his denying burial for Polyneices he "wronged the nether gods" (*Antigone* 1070).

The Greek belief that no human corpse should be left unburied is also mentioned by the early second-century writer Aelian. He wrote, "Anyone who came across an unburied body was obliged to cover it with earth and to bury it facing west" (*Varia Historia* 5:14). Some additional Greek literature indicates the strong Greek desire to leave no dead person unburied, not covered with earth, was also motivated by the belief that an unburied-dead person would not enter the mythological Elysian Fields (*Elysii Campi*) where the dead went to experience eternal pleasures.

The fear of nonburial was not confined to Greeks. The ancient Hebrews also feared it. The prophet Jeremiah noted with horror dead people not buried. To be unburied was equivalent to being garbage or refuse (Jeremiah 25:33). The horror of not being interred is also stated in the New Testament (Revelation 11:9).

Some historical records show that among the Romans, who for centuries had consigned their dead to earth burial, cremation began to be practiced about the mid-seventh century before Christ. Cicero, however, implies it began much later, namely in the first century BC, with Lucius Cornelius Sulla who died in 68 BC. Sulla, a Roman general and dictator, ordered that when he died, his body was to be burned, apparently because he feared someone might do to him what he had done to Gaius Marius (also a general), whom he exhumed and then dispersed his body parts (*De legibus* 2:57). Cicero's observation is similar to Pliny the Elder's statement that says: "Cremation was not actually an old practice at Rome: the dead used to be buried. But cremation was instituted after it became known that the bodies of those fallen in wars abroad were dug up again" (*Natural History* 7:187).

Although cremation was widespread in ancient Rome, most Romans were not cremated. For the most part only those of high political status or wealthy citizens could afford cremation. But not all higher-status individuals necessarily opted for cremation, for Plutarch in his work *Parallel Lives* mentions that Numa, the legendary king of Rome in the seventh century BC, ordered that his body not be cremated. He was entombed in a stone coffin (*Solon* 22).

It is also important to note that the poor and the slaves who comprised the bulk of the Roman population were not cremated. Often, these social outcasts, *infamia*, as the Romans called them, were either buried in common pits (*puticuli*)[16] or left lying on roadsides. Social outcasts and the poor could not afford the fuel (mostly costly cypress wood) along with the unguents to preserve the body for three days before it was incinerated.[17] For those who were cremated, columbaria (where cinerary urns were kept with cremated remains) were sometimes constructed (about twenty years before Christ) so that the urns containing the burned remains (ashes and unburned bones) could be deposited. However, it is important to remember that only a few Roman cities or towns had columbaria.[18]

Cremation was also practiced in some other parts of the West, before and outside the Roman Empire. From about 1500 till 1800 BC, the Nordic culture of Scandinavia, for example, performed crematory acts on fire boats. Each boat was outfitted with a funeral pyre, and after the survivors ignited the boat, it was set adrift on the sea.[19]

Although cremation has a pagan origin, not all pagans practiced it at the same time in history, and some pagans never practiced it. For instance, the ancient Egyptians and some Chinese chose not to cremate their dead. Apparently the Hindus practiced it before most other pagan societies. In Japan it became fashionable with Buddhism's appearance in the sixth century BC.

Cremating Dead Husbands and Live Widows

Most commonly, when the cremation of human bodies is mentioned, people tend to think that the bodies being cremated are dead. However, among the Hindus in India, cremation often involved more than just the deceased person. For more than two thousand years, India practiced *sati* (or *suttee*), a religious rite of Hindus who burned not just the body of a woman's dead husband but also his live widow. The soldiers of Alexander the Great found *sati* prevalent in Panjab already in the fourth century BC.[20]

When an Indian husband died, his wife, as a good and faithful Hindu, was expected to mount her husband's funeral pyre voluntarily and submit herself to be burned with him. If she refused, she was usually put there by force, often by her sons or other family members. If she managed to elude this pagan institution, her life in society was socially ruined. She would be treated as a nonperson, not just because she evaded her husband's funeral pyre but also because among the Hindus in India a widow was culturally and religiously despised. She could only eat one meal per day, perform only menial tasks, and wear the dowdiest of clothes. She could no longer sleep in a bed. Her head had to be shaved monthly so she was conspicuous as well as being undesirable to promiscuous men. Religious ceremonies and weddings were off limits to her. She could not be seen by a pregnant woman because a simple glance might bring a curse to her pregnancy or to her unborn child.[21] Not infrequently, as a result of India's child-bride custom, a widow was burned while she still was a child, between the ages of five and fifteen.[22] In some instances when the deceased husband was buried rather than cremated, the widow was not burned alive but buried alive with her husband in his grave.[23]

It needs to be noted that before the Hindu widow mounted her husband's funeral pyre, dressed in bridal finery, she would walk at the head of the funeral procession leading to the place of cremation.[24] The pomp of the procession and its accompanying noise of applause of on-looking women often produced a "psychological intoxication [that boosted the widow's courage] till she had passed beyond the reach of succor."[25]

As a result of Christianity's longstanding respect for women and its concern for the welfare of widows, the British authorities in 1829, under the suasion of Governor-General William Bentinck, outlawed the practice of *sati*. When the ban went into effect, many (mostly women) "cried that the foundations of Hindu society would be shaken if widows were not burnt alive."[26] Others argued the ban violated Article XXV of India's constitution that gave the people freedom of religion.[27] But the British, swayed by Christian values, were not deterred, for in 1856 Indian widows were even granted another basic human right: the right to remarry.[28]

Questions are sometimes asked, such as, "How and why did *sati* originate in the Hindu religion of India?" One explanation says it arose because Hindu husbands feared their wives, when angry at them, would poison them. So in order to protect themselves from the imagined danger, they introduced *sati*. It would deter a wife from killing her husband, knowing that if she poisoned him, she would have to die with him too, so she would gain nothing by killing him. Moreover, if she did kill him and somehow managed to escape *sati*, her life as a widow (already noted) would be worse than that of a prostitute or pariah.[29] She would even be ostracized by her immediate family.

Pagan India was not alone in burning live widows. History shows that widows were once burned in pre-Christianized Scandinavia and among the Chinese, the Finns, and the Maori in New Zealand. A few American Indian tribes also burned their widows alive.[30]

Cremation in the New World before Columbus

Research shows cremating the dead was practiced by some of the aborigines in Australia. Estimates indicate the aborigines in Australia began burning their dead about the time of Christ's birth,[31] roughly two millennia after cremation began in the ancient world of India. In North America some American Indians, as already noted, also cremated their dead. These aborigines lived mostly in the Yukon, Washington, California, and Great Basin area. When they began cremating their dead is not really known.

In light of recent publicity and new American federal laws, especially since the early 1990s when the "Native American Graves Protection and Repatriation Act" was enacted by the US Congress, concentrated efforts have been made (and still are) to bury all human skeletons of American Indians, many of which have been on display for decades in various museums. Today, many American Indians are demanding that all human skeletons be returned to them so they can bury them. These demands have led many Indians and also non-Indians erroneously to conclude that all Indians in the past (before Europeans came to America) interred their dead, similar to what most Europeans and Americans did as a result of their Judeo-Christian background. This assumption, however, is incorrect because historical research reveals that of the approximately three hundred American Indians tribes in existence at the time of Columbus, many Indians did not bury their dead, as indicated above.

In addition to inhumation and cremation, some American Indians disposed of their dead in a variety of other ways. In much of the Midwest and the Great Plains of the United States, many tribes placed their dead on crudely constructed scaffolds (platforms) where they slowly decomposed, along with vultures feeding on them. As the corpse lost its flesh, the bones were often flexed and placed in a bone hovel. The Teton Dakotas, on the other hand, wrapped the corpse in cloth and then wedged the body into the fork of a tree. Here predators soon ate the body's flesh. In the southeastern United States, the Choctaw Indians removed the flesh from their dead and then kept the bones in a bone hut. In parts of Tennessee and Alabama the Indians of the Alexander Culture (AD 500–900) buried many of their deceased in refuse piles. Some of the Pueblo Indians (AD 700–900) also placed their dead in mounds of refuse.[32] The Ponca Indians initially placed their deceased on elevated scaffolds but later, as a result of European influence, buried them.

Other tribes, for instance, some on the Northwest coast, left their dead to dogs and wolves. This practice sometimes also occurred in other parts of the continent. For instance, in 1632 Thomas Morton in his book *The New English Canaan* wrote: "In times of general Mortality they [some northeastern Indian tribes] omit the Ceremonies of burying, exposing the dead Carkases [sic] to the

Beasts of prey ..."[33] In speaking about some Indians in the arctic, Harold E. Driver, the renowned expert on American Indian life, found similar funeral practices among some other tribes. "In the arctic the dead were most often left on the surface of the ground, because it was impractical to dig a grave [with a digging stick] in the frozen soil, and there were no trees to provide poles for a raised scaffold or wood for a crematory fire."[34]

Although most American Indians did not cremate their dead, it would be a mistake to conclude (as already noted) that all those who did not cremate their deceased buried them. And even with those who did practice earth burial, especially after the Europeans had arrived in America, another fact needs to be kept in mind. "Christian missionaries everywhere encouraged burial in the ground [therefore] it is difficult to decide how much inhumation ... is native and how much is European."[35]

Ancient Egypt and China

Although cremation originated in pagan societies, not all pagans chose to burn their deceased members, as already shown. One well-known ancient group of people who did not subject their deceased to consuming flames were the Egyptians, for they believed cremating the dead destroyed the realization of an afterlife for them.[36] The Egyptians apparently honored the dead so much that they originated and developed the art of embalming/mummifying in order to preserve the deceased body. This process evidently was already practiced at least by the beginning of the second millennium before Christ, for we find that Joseph (a Hebrew and a high-ranking official in the Egyptian government) ordered his physicians to embalm/mummify his dead father Jacob (Genesis 50:2), who, as the result of seven years of drought and famine, had come from Canaan to avoid starvation. Later, when Joseph died, he too was embalmed, and they also placed him into a coffin (Genesis 50:26).

In the past, ancient China has often been cited as not having cremated its deceased. But contrary to these citations, Marco Polo (d. ca. 1324), the medieval Italian traveler, found that the Chinese did practice cremation in some of their provinces.[37] Today, cremation is no longer confined to a few Chinese provinces but is widespread throughout the country. In 2010, China cremated 49 percent of its deceased residents.[38] Scattering the ashes of the deceased is now quite fashionable, as well.[39]

In addition to the Egyptians, the ancient Hebrews, from the time of Abraham to Jesus Christ, also did not cremate their dead. As shown in chapter 3, they spurned cremation not simply because it was a pagan practice but because paganism denied the physical resurrection of the body, and they did not want to be identified with a practice that was contrary to this vital doctrine. Thus, when they entered the Promised Land (Canaan) after their exodus from Egypt, God warned them repeatedly not to imitate or adopt their pagan neighbors' religious beliefs and practices, clearly stated in Deuteronomy 6 and 7.

Conclusion

Although cremation began with pagan religious groups, not all pagans burned their dead. The ancient Egyptians were one such society. Cremating the dead by pagans was commonly interwoven with varying religious beliefs regarding the deceased individual's soul. Many groups believed that cremating the body freed or released the soul from the body in which it had been held captive during the person's life. One cannot help but wonder if any pagan groups would have practiced cremation if they had believed in a future resurrection of the human body, rather than only in the survivability of the soul.

It was pagan religious beliefs associated with cremating the dead that in part made cremation repugnant to the ancient Hebrews and later also to the early Christians in Rome. Chapter 3 discusses how pagan beliefs conflicted with the biblical views of the Hebrews, and the sixth chapter shows why the early Christians consistently spurned cremation.

---

[1] John Jamieson, "On the Origin of Cremation," *The Transactions of the Royal Society of Edinburgh* (1818), 8: 83.

[2] Robin Lane Fox, *Pagans and Christians* (San Francisco, CA: Perennial Library, 1988), 31.

[3] Roger Bacon, *The Opus Majus*, trans. Robert Belle Burke (New York: Russell and Russell, 1962), 792.

[4] Ramsay MacMullen, *Christianizing the Roman Empire, A.D. 100-400* (New Haven, CT: Yale University Press, 1984), 116.

[5] Fox, op. cit., 31.

[6] Stephen Prothero, *Purified by Fire: A History of Cremation in America* (Berkeley, CA: University of California Press, 2001), 6.

[7] E. Rohde, *The Cult of the Soul and Belief in Immortality Among the Greeks* (London: Routledge and Kegan Paul, 1950), 21.

[8] Prothero, op. cit., 6.

[9] William Howells, *The Heathens: Primitive Man and His Religions* (Garden City, NY: Doubleday and Company, 1948), 158.

[10] Jay Miller, "Ashes Ethereal: Cremation in the Americas," *American Indian Culture and Research Journal* (2001), 131.

[11] Ibid., 126.

[12] Ibid., 123.

[13] Ibid., 124.

[14] Howells, op. cit., 158.

[15] C. J. Polson (ed.) *The Disposal of the Dead* (New York: Philosophical Library, 1953), 83.

[16] Disposing of human corpses in the *puticuli* is further discussed in chapter 8.

[17] T.G. Tucker, *Life in the Roman World of Nero and St. Paul* (New York: Macmillan and Company, 1929), 446.

[18] Rodolfo Lanciani, *Pagan and Christian Rome* (Boston: Houghton Mifflin and Company, 1892), 256.

[19] Paul E. Irion, *Cremation* (Philadelphia, PA: Fortress Press, 1968), 17.

[20] Edward Thompson, *Suttee: A Historical and Philosophical Enquiry into the Hindu Rite of Widow Burning* (London: Allen and Unwin, 1928), 19.

[21] Katherine Mayo, *Mother India* (New York: Blue Ribbon Books, 1927), 73.

22 Monica Felton, *A Child Widow's Story* (New York: Harcourt, Brace, and World, 1966), 69.

23 H. G. Rawlinson, *India: A Short Cultural History* (New York: Frederick A. Praeger, 1952), 279.

24 Sakuntala Narasimhan, *Sati: Widow Burning in India* (New York: Anchor Books, 1990), 2.

25 Thompson, op. cit., 50.

26 Rawlinson, op. cit., 279.

27 Narasimhan, op. cit., 4.

28 Stanley Wolpert, *A New History of India* (New York: Oxford University Press, 2000), 233.

29 Mayo, op. cit., 83.

30 Dorothy K. Stein, "Women to Burn: Suttee as a Normative Institution," *Signs: Journal of Women, Culture, and Society* (Winter, 1978), 253.

31 Kenneth V. Iserson, *Death To Dust: What Happens to the Dead Bodies* (Tucson, AZ: Galen Press, 1994), 237.

32 Paul S. Martin, et al., *Indians Before Columbus* (Chicago: University of Chicago Press, 1947), 287.

33 Thomas Morton, *The New English Canaan* (New York: Burt Frankline, 1883 [1632]), 171.

34 Harold E. Driver, *Indians of North America* (Chicago: University of Chicago Press, 1961), 448–49.

35 Ibid., 449.

36 Iserson, op. cit., 238.

37 Thomas Wright (ed.), *The Travels of Marco Polo*, trans. Marsden revised (London: Henry G. Bohn, 1854), 214, 283.

38 "International Cremation Statistics 2010," *Pharos International* (Winter 2011), 27.

39 Anonymous, "The World's Way of Death," *The Economist* (November 14, 1998), 95.

CHAPTER 3

HEBREWS REJECTED CREMATION

When you come into the land the Lord your God is giving you, you shall not learn to follow the abominable practices of those nations.
—Deuteronomy 18:9

God's people, the Hebrews (Israelites) in the Old Testament era, were surrounded by pagan cultures: the Canaanites, the Amorites, the Edomites, the Hittites, the Philistines, and others. Through his prophets, God frequently warned the Hebrews not to adopt the pagan values, beliefs, or practices of their neighboring cultures. They were commanded not to worship polytheistic gods, not to marry pagan wives, not to engage in homosexual practices, not to eat unclean food, not to sacrifice infants, not to make graven images of pagan idols, and not to follow other pagan customs.

Throughout the Old Testament there is a marked theological *Sitz-im-leben* that shows cremation was not how God wanted his people to dispose of their dead. Even some pagan writers were conscious of this Hebrew norm. For instance, the Roman writer Tacitus (ca. AD 56–120) wrote that the Hebrews "bury rather than burn dead bodies" (*The Histories* 5:5).

Burial of Abraham and His Descendants

The first earth burial without embalmment recorded in the Old Testament is that of Abraham's wife Sarah. When she died, Abraham wanted an honorable place to bury her, so he approached Ephron, a Hittite, about purchasing the field of Machpelah in the district of Hebron. After acquiring the land for four hundred shekels, he buried Sarah in one of the field's caves (Genesis 23:19). Later, when Abraham died, he too had himself laid to rest there. It was also here where Abraham's son Isaac, "being old and full of days," later was interred by his two sons Esau and Jacob (Genesis 35:29). And Isaac's wife, Rebekah, who with her son Jacob deceived her husband for Esau's birthright, lies buried here too (Genesis 49:31).

The interments of Abraham and his son Isaac draw no particular attention, but later the death and burial of Jacob, the grandson of Abraham, does. Some years before Jacob died, seven years of severe famine struck the land of Canaan. Early in the course of the famine, Jacob heard that neighboring Egypt had plenty of grain. This was the result of prudent planning by a wise official in Egypt during the seven years of plenty that preceded the famine. Unknown to Jacob, this wise official was his son Joseph. His jealous, conniving brothers some years earlier had sold him for twenty shekels to a traveling caravan that took him to Egypt and then deceitfully told their father that a wild animal had killed him. With the famine pressing upon Jacob and his sons, Jacob commanded his ten sons to travel to Egypt and bring back some grain so they would avoid starvation. Soon Jacob sent his sons on a second trip to Egypt. Upon their arrival this time, Joseph identified himself and invited his brothers, their families, and his father Jacob to migrate to Egypt so that they would no longer be burdened by the remaining years of the seven-year famine.

Just before Jacob died in Egypt, Joseph heard his father request, "Bury me with my fathers in the cave in the field of Ephron the Hittite" (Genesis 49:29). So when Jacob died, Joseph, in keeping with his father's request, asked Pharaoh, his superior, for permission to take his father's bones to Canaan for burial, and Pharaoh granted his wish. Joseph and a large entourage took Jacob's body back to his homeland, where they buried him in the same field where Abraham and Sarah had been laid to rest (Genesis 50:5–6, 13). Interestingly, Jacob had buried his first wife, Leah, on this same plot of ground before he migrated to Egypt (Genesis 49:31).

Jacob's request to be buried in his homeland, even though it was tremendously inconvenient for Joseph and all who accompanied him on their long trip to Canaan, indicates that it was inconceivable to him that his body could be disposed of in any other way than by earth burial. Had his body been cremated, the task of transporting his remains over desert territory, for several hundreds of miles, would have eased the burden of this long journey significantly. Some, however, might say that Jacob's desire not only reflected a Hebrew norm but one that also received additional support from Egypt's culture, for the Egyptians embalmed/mummified and later buried their dead rather than burn them, as was done in many other societies. The basis of Jacob's desire to be buried goes back not only to Abraham but even to Adam. For instance, shortly after Adam's fall into sin, God told him that he would die someday, and his body created from the dust of the earth would eventually return to dust (Genesis 3:19). These words, spoken soon after Adam's fall, are a clear indication that God's plan for a deceased human body is to bury it in an earthen grave. Thus, A. W. Argyle asserts, "Divine ordinance required the human flesh should return to dust, not ashes, that is, it should be buried."[1]

Jacob's desire to be buried in Canaan was later imitated by his son Joseph. He, like his father, obtained a promise under oath that his bones would someday be taken to Canaan, the land promised to Abraham and his descendants (Genesis 50:24-25). Then some three hundred years after Joseph's death, when Moses led the Israelites out of Egypt to the land of Canaan, we read,

"Moses took the bones of Joseph with him ..." (Exodus 13:19). At first thought, the transporting of Joseph's bones may not seem like much, but it is helpful to remember that the trek across the wilderness to the Promised Land took forty years. Thus, for two-score years the Israelites carried and protected his bones during this time until they buried them in Shechem on a plot of ground his father Jacob had purchased before he went to Egypt to join his son (Joshua 24:32).

The transporting of Joseph's bones for forty arduous years enables biblically grounded opponents of cremation to argue that this determined act by the Israelites underscores the great importance God's people placed on earth burial and by their transporting Joseph's bones, they conformed to God's will. This argument receives support when one recalls that when Moses died, God himself buried him. The biblical text reads, "So Moses the servant of the Lord died there in land of Moab ... and he [God] buried him in the valley in the land Moab opposite Beth Peor, but no one knows the place of his burial to this day" (Deuteronomy 34:5–6).

Christians who think cremation is an acceptable option and that God has no objections regarding it may want to ask why God himself buried Moses in an earthen grave. By giving Moses an earth burial, did God perhaps intend to show his people that he only approves of their placing a deceased friend or relative in the bosom of the earth? Biblically informed opponents of cremation can respond by saying yes. Here an affirmative statement from the rabbinic oral law (ca. 500 BC to AD 200) comes to mind. "Follow the path of God ... bury the dead, even as he [God] did bury Moses in the valley of Moab" (Sotah 14a).

During the centuries after Moses, the Hebrews continued to inter their dead. The Bible's biographies of numerous individuals commonly end with mention of their being buried. Thus, after the Exodus from Egypt, the wear and tear of one hundred ten years took the life of Joshua, the successor to Moses, and he, like his forefathers, was laid to rest in a grave (Joshua 24:30). Samuel, the man of God who anointed both King Saul and his successor King David, died and was buried at his home in Ramah (1 Samuel 25:1). And when King David's time had come to depart, he was buried in the city of David, Jerusalem (1 Kings 2:10). Many other noteworthy individuals, too numerous to name, are mentioned in the pages of the Old Testament as receiving earth burial. So important was inhumation to the Hebrews that they even buried the slain bodies of their enemies (1 Kings 11:15). Then, almost a thousand years after the Exodus, the apocryphal book Tobit, written during the Babylonian exile in the sixth century BC, reports that the Hebrews also buried strangers (Tobit 1:17–18). The biblical ethic of giving burial to indigent people was still practiced at the time of Christ, when, for instance, there existed in Jerusalem the potter's field, primarily a burial site for the poor and strangers (Matthew 27:7).

Cremation as Divine Punishment

After the Israelites had returned from Egypt, they continued to bury their dead, and when they did cremate some people, it was primarily a form of punishment for those who had committed heinous acts. Thus, Joshua announced that the transgressor "shall be burned with fire, he and all that he has, because he has transgressed the covenant of the Lord, and because he has done an outrageous thing in Israel" (Joshua 7:15). Moses commanded the punishment of a consuming fire for a daughter of a priest who profaned herself and her father by engaging in prostitution (Leviticus 21:9). For another grievously sinful act Moses stated, "If a man marries a woman and her mother, it is wickedness. They shall be burned with fire, both he and they, that there may be no wickedness among you" (Leviticus 20:14 NKJV). Moses also punished Nadab and Abihu, two sons of Aaron, by burning them for having offered unauthorized incense and fire to the Lord (Leviticus 10:1–2).

But not all violators or criminals, not even some who were guilty of capital crimes, were always cremated under the Old Testament's justice system. Most criminals, it seems, were simply executed and then buried. This is evident from the words Moses spoke concerning criminals who had been executed by hanging. The text reads, "His body shall not remain on the tree, but you shall surely bury him the same day, for a hanged man is cursed by God" (Deuteronomy 21:23). This reference indicates the Israelites generally buried rather than cremated most criminals. Interestingly, this is also how Jewish rabbis in the era of oral law understood this reference in Deuteronomy. For the Talmud cites this Deuteronomy passage that says if anyone seeks to dispose of a human corpse other than by inhumation, his wishes must be rejected (Sanhedrin 46b).

Cremation: Instrument of God's Wrath

In addition to the Hebrews being directed by God to cremate some criminals in the flames of fire as a sign to others as punishment and humiliation, God at times also used fire to show and exercise his holy wrath, especially when people spurned his divine will. While on their way to the Promised Land, some Israelites angrily and publicly complained. This act displeased the Lord, prompting him to consume them by fire (Numbers 11:1). Also, during the Exodus journey, Korah and two hundred fifty conspiring Levites, who rebelled against Moses and Aaron by burning incense at the door of the tabernacle, were consumed by the Lord's fire (Numbers 16:35). And after the Israelites had arrived in the Promised Land, Achan ("the troubler of Israel") was stoned and burned, together with his family, for stealing and hiding silver, gold, and other items taken as booty against God's will from the fallen city of Jericho (Joshua 7:15, 24–26). In the ninth century BC, Elijah called upon God to send fire from heaven to consume King Ahaziah's two groups of fifty men each, along with two captains (2 Kings 1:10–12), and God granted his request.

The use of fire to purge evil and to avenge God's anger is also evident in the well-known golden calf incident. After Moses descended from Mount Sinai, he, as God's representative, angrily began to destroy this idol by first burning it. Next, he ground it to powder, mixed it with water, and then had some Israelites drink it (Exodus 32:20). On another occasion, Moses ordered the Israelites to burn all of their pagan neighbors' carved images of man-made gods (Deuteronomy 7:25). And one of the best-known acts that illustrates God's use of fire as an instrument of his wrath is his total destruction of Sodom and Gomorrah (Genesis 19:24). These Old Testament incidents show cremating human bodies at times was done specifically to purge evildoers in Israel who violated God's will and holy Law.

Cremation: A Great Sin in God's Eyes

Throughout the entire Old Testament, the act of destroying deceased humans by fire was never pleasing to God. This is especially evident with regard to the king of Moab, who took the bones from the king of Edom's tomb and burned them to lime. In response to this act, God had the prophet Amos declare, "This is what the Lord says, 'For three transgressions of Moab, and for four, I will not revoke the punishment, because he burned to lime the bones of the king of Edom. So I will send a fire upon Moab, and it shall devour the strongholds of Kerioth [a city], and Moab shall die amid the uproar" (Amos 2:1–2).

It is noteworthy that this Amos account focuses only on what the Moabite king did to Edom's king, a pagan king, not a king of Israel. Yet God took great offense regarding Moab's act of cremating the king of Edom. A heathen king cremating a heathen king did not minimize the gravity of what he did. The offense was so great that God sent fire to destroy King Moab and his fortresses. God gave him a dose of his own medicine. He fought fire with fire.

He did not tolerate cremation even for a pagan king. Hence, it can be argued that this biblical reference in Amos 2:1–2 is a clear denunciation of cremation, one that applies to heathen and God's people alike. As James Fraser, a Christian opposed to cremation, has noted regarding this passage in Amos, "If there is any verse in the Bible that positively emphasizes God's disapproval of the burning of human bodies, it is this."[2]

Cremation Is Not for God's People

That God does not want people, especially those who love and fear him, to be cremated is apparent when the words and acts of King Josiah (seventh century BC) are considered. Josiah went to the town of Bethel, where he engaged in the task of burning wooden idols and pagan altars, as well as burning the bones of the pagan Baal priests (2 Kings 23:16, 20; 2 Chronicles 34:5). In the process of burning them, he came upon one particular tomb; intent on cremating its remains, he enquired whose tomb it was. Some of the Bethel men told him that it contained the bones of a "man of God who came from Judah" (2 Kings 23:17), a man who had condemned the pagan altars, just as Josiah now was doing. Upon hearing this, he said, "Let him be; let no man move his bones" (2 Kings 23:18). The remains of this God-fearing man were not to be burned. Josiah's words, similar to those uttered by the prophet Amos, provide additional evidence that in the Old Testament it was not people faithful to God who were burned but those who had provoked his holy wrath.

Old Testament's View of a Human Corpse

The dignity of the human body was one reason the Hebrews rejected cremation. To dispose of the deceased human by burning was considered "a rejection of the concept of *kevod ha-met* [respect due to the deceased]. To commit the body to destruction by fire was tantamount to the deliberate burning of something that once was sacred."[3]

The strong opposition to cremation by the Hebrews in the Old Testament era is especially significant when we remember that they had a number of taboos regarding the human corpse, particularly as it concerned priests. The high priest, for instance, was not to go near a dead human body (Leviticus 21:11). If he did, he had to purify himself by washing his body with water, and he was not clean until after sunset (Leviticus 22:6–7). Another prohibition, spelled out during the Exodus from Egypt to the Promised Land, stated, "Whoever touches the dead body of any person shall be unclean for seven days" (Numbers 19:11). Such ritually unclean persons had to purify themselves by using running (spring) water mixed with the ashes of a red heifer sprinkled on them by a ritually clean person (Numbers 19:17–22).

In spite of individuals being prone to uncleanness through physical contact with a deceased person, the Hebrews nevertheless treated the dead person with great respect. It was customary for someone in the immediate family, usually a son, to close the eyes of his departed parent. This was what Joseph did to his father, Jacob, in Egypt (Genesis 46:4). The body was also washed, as was done to Tabitha (Dorcas) when she died (Acts 9:37). In addition, a napkin was draped over the person's face (John 11:44). Then the person was anointed with aromatic spices and wrapped in linen materials (*Shabbat* 23:5). Wrapped in linen, the deceased body was commonly carried on a bier to an earth depression or pit, usually within twenty-four hours, without embalmment. The Old Testament makes mention of a coffin only once, namely, that of Joseph in Egypt (Genesis 50:26). The Egyptians apparently used coffins, whereas the Hebrews did not.

After the Hebrews had laid a corpse into a pit in the earth, it was commonly covered with a heap of stones.[4] King David's rebellious son Absalom was buried in that manner. "They took Absalom and threw him into a great pit in the forest and raised over him a very large heap of stones" (2 Samuel 18:17). The stones were placed over the pit or grave to prevent wild animals from getting to the corpse. After one year or so, when the flesh of the body had decayed, the bones were then taken from a pit or from a cave and placed in a tomb or in a limestone ossuary.[5] An ossuary of this kind recently became known to the public in October of 2002. It bears the inscription "James, Brother of Jesus,"[6] possibly the half-brother of Jesus.

Similar to the ancient Greeks (noted in the previous chapter), not to give a deceased person earth burial was inconceivable, a curse in the eyes of the Hebrews. That kind of curse was predicted for King Jehoiakim. God had the prophet Jeremiah announce that not only would the Babylonians destroy and devastate his country's land, but his "dead shall be cast out to the heat by day and the frost by the night" (Jeremiah 36:29–30). And Ecclesiastes 6:3 asserts that a stillborn infant is more fortunate than a person who receives no burial.

The Burning of King Saul and His Sons

A couple of decades ago, a Christian theologian, John J. Davis, published his book (*What About Cremation? A Christian Perspective*, 1989). In part, Davis asks whether cremation may be practiced by Christians. Although he does not favor cremation, he nevertheless states, "There are two instances in the Old Testament where bodies appear to have been cremated under favorable or acceptable conditions."[7] His first example is the cremation of King Saul and his three sons who were burned by the inhabitants of Jabesh-gilead after the Philistines had killed them and fastened the king's body to the wall of Beth Shan (1 Samuel 31:11–12). After the Jabesh men had burned the bodies of King Saul and his three sons, they buried their bones "under the tamarisk tree in Jabesh" (1 Samuel 31:13).

When Davis says burning King Saul and his three sons is an acceptable example of a Hebrew cremation, he exceeds the plain wording of the biblical text. For one must ask, to whom was this act of cremation acceptable? There is no evidence in the text that it was acceptable to anyone, and certainly not to God. Perhaps it was acceptable to the men who did the burning, for they evidently did not want Saul and his dead sons to be further abused by the Philistines who had decapitated him after they found him dead. Thus, not only is there no evidence to see this cremation incident as biblically acceptable to God, but it also is not an act Christians or anyone else may cite to justify or defend cremation. That the burning of King Saul's body is mentioned in the Bible does not make it acceptable. It is simply a descriptive account, not one that has prescriptive import.

It should further be noted that only the flesh of these four bodies (Saul and his three sons) was burned, for the biblical text (as noted above) states their bones were later "buried ... under the tamarisk tree at Jabesh" (1 Samuel 31:13). It is also important to remember another biblical reference states after the unburned bones of Saul and his sons were buried, "God responded to the plea [prayer] for the land" (2 Samuel 21:14). Thus, the burying of the charred bones of King Saul and those of his sons provides additional evidence that God wants his people laid to rest in the bosom of the earth rather than subjected to destructive flames of fire. Thus, Davis's citing Saul's and his sons' cremation in support of cremation today has no merit.

Cremation in Samaria

The second Hebrew example Davis cites from the Bible as favorable to cremation is the account cited by the prophet Amos. That account reads, "And when a relative of the dead, with one who will burn the bodies, picks up the bodies to take them out of the house, he will say to the one inside the house, 'Are there any more with you?' Then someone will say, 'None.' And he will say, 'Hold your tongue! For we dare not mention the name of the Lord.'" (Amos 6:10). Here we must question whether these words can really be understood as being favorable to cremation. The context seems to indicate that they speak about the consequences of a future pestilence—a judgment of God—that would cause numerous deaths as a result of the Assyrian Empire's military siege, and that burning these multiple dead bodies would prevent "the air from being polluted by the decomposition of the corpses."[8] Hence, the words of Amos do not say, nor do they imply, that cremation is an acceptable way for God's people to dispose of their dead.

Cremation: A Form of Idolatry

In light of the unholy background of cremation in the Old Testament, it is not surprising that rabbis in the oral law period not only saw it as an unacceptable way to dispose of their dead, but they also believed it to be a practice synonymous with idolatry. Thus, the Talmud, the formal codification of the oral law, boldly states, "Every death which is accompanied by burning is looked upon as idolatry" (*Avodah Zarah* 1:3).

To be sure, the Talmud is extrabiblical (noncanonical) religious literature, but if it saw cremation as a form of idolatry, then the same condemnations that God in the Old Testament directed against other idolatrous acts may also be applied to the practice of cremation.

Even though the idolatrous view of cremation in the Talmud is not a citation from the Old Testament, it seems to reflect the many negative views the Old Testament expressed concerning the burning of deceased humans. In short, the Talmudic reference provides additional evidence that cremation was unthinkable and unacceptable to faithful Hebrews.

The Luz Bone Argument

A discussion of the Hebrew or Jewish view of cremation would not be complete without mentioning the concept of the Luz bone that some rabbis called the "resurrection bone." Exactly when the extrabiblical concept of the Luz bone appeared is difficult to ascertain, but it is found in the Talmudic literature. Although the Luz bone has been important to many Jews from the rabbinic era on with regard to the resurrection of the body, there has been uncertainty as to this bone's exact location. Some think it is the coccyx (a small bone at the base of the spine), and others believe it is the bone at the back of the human skull.

Some Orthodox rabbis think the Luz bone is reason to oppose cremation because they say fire would destroy it and hence prevent the incinerated person from being resurrected. One rabbinic source declares, "With cremation that bone can be destroyed and the resurrection stymied."[9] On the other hand, the Midrash, another rabbinic source, notes that this bone cannot be destroyed even by fire. Rabbi Joshua Hanania demonstrated this to a skeptic. According to the Midrash, "He threw it into the fire, yet it was not burnt; he put it in water, but it did not dissolve; he ground it between two millstones, but it was not crushed; he placed it on an anvil and smote it with a hammer; the anvil was cleft and the hammer split, yet it remained intact" (*Bereshith Rabbah* 28:3). Whether the Luz bone is destructible or not, or whether there is such a bone, it reveals that rabbis in the rabbinic period, even after the formation of the Old Testament canon, continued to uphold and defend earth burial as the only acceptable way to dispose of dead human beings.

Modern Judaism's Cremation Views

The long-standing wall of opposition to cremation, so characteristic of the Hebrews in the Old Testament and in the rabbinic era, has in recent years begun to crack as some of their descendants today are beginning to choose cremation. Of the three main bodies of Judaism (Orthodox, Conservative, and Reformed), the Orthodox Jews have been the strongest opponents of cremation, while the Conservatives have been less opposed, and the Reformed have offered the least resistance. In recent years, however, the forces of secularism have begun to make significant inroads into all three Jewish groups. Thus, even the Orthodox United Synagogue in London, England, for example, now gives permission for cremation if there is a normal funeral ceremony and if the ashes will be buried in a casket.[10] However, in the United States Orthodox Jews, especially as represented by the Hasidic and Chabad Chassidism branches, are still strongly opposed to cremation and permit no exception. The latter two groups value the Luz-bone argument.

Recently, some Orthodox rabbis have posted articles on the Internet voicing their opposition to cremation. One such posting, by Rabbi Y. M. Tuchichinsky, on the Internet's topic of "Ask the Rabbi," responded to an inquiry about cremation as follows: "According to Jewish law, one should not '*sit shiva*' (observe Jewish mourning rites) for someone who has been cremated voluntarily, nor is one obliged to bury their [sic] ashes." This rabbi continued, "In addition, the body of a voluntarily cremated person is not liable for resurrection; this is not so much because of the physical impediment, but rather in line with the concept that one who doesn't believe in resurrection will not experience it."[11]

This latter argument, however, has no biblical support. For according to the Old and New Testament, one's bodily resurrection is not dependent on the person's faith in the resurrection. The prophet Daniel made this quite clear. "And many of those who sleep in the dust of the earth shall awake, some to everlasting life, and some to shame and everlasting contempt" (Daniel 12:2). Similarly, the apostle John cites Jesus saying, "[For] an hour is coming when all who are in the tombs will hear his voice and come out. Those who have done good to the resurrection of life, and those who have done evil to the resurrection of judgment" (John 5:28–29).

With regard to Conservative Jews, the Law Committee of the Conservative Rabbinical Assembly in the United States has given a green light to its rabbis to conduct funerals for cremated members—that is, if they are cremated after the funeral ceremony.[12] The Reformed Jews, although they do not encourage cremation, appear to have little or no problem with it, and some are now choosing this method.

Conclusion

Although God at times used fire to punish and destroy grievous evildoers, either by employing intermediaries or by directly using it himself, there is not a single indication in the entire Old Testament that God ever wanted cremation used as an alternative to earth burial, for instance, for noncriminals or for his faithful people. Nor is there any evidence in the Old Testament that burning even wicked people pleased God. For he says, "I have no pleasure in the death of the wicked" (Ezekiel 33:11). This being true, it would appear that he also takes no pleasure in seeing the wicked being incinerated, even when on some occasions he himself commanded it for some criminals.

Finally, it should be noted that in ancient Palestine, where the climate brought about a rapid decomposition of a deceased body, it would have made sense for the Hebrews to burn their dead, but they did not. Why not? Because they knew such behavior was contrary to the will of God, who, either himself or through his prophets, used cremation only as a form of punishment and humiliation for individuals who were guilty of the most notorious sins or crimes. It is also important to note that none of the relatively few cremation instances found in the Old Testament ever had God's blessings. Rather, most cremations mentioned in the Old Testament are examples of punishment handed out to individuals who violated God's law(s).

---

[1] A. W. Argyle, "The Historical Christian Attitude to Cremation," *The Hibbert Journal* (October, 1958), 68.

[2] James W. Fraser, *Cremation: Is It Christian?* (Neptune, NJ: Loizeaux Brothers, 1965), 14.

3   Chaim Pearl, "Cremation," *The Oxford Dictionary of the Jewish Religion* (New York: The Oxford University Press, 1997), 181.

4   J. B. Payne, "Burial," *The International Standard Bible Encyclopedia* (Grand Rapids, MI: Eerdmans Publishing Company, 1956), 1: 557.

5   Andre Lemaire, "Burial Box of James the Brother of Jesus," *Biblical Archaeology* (November/December, 2002), 26.

6   Ibid.

7   John J. Davis, *What About Cremation? A Christian Perspective* (Winona Lake, IN: BMH Books, 1989), 66.

8   C. F. Keil, *Commentary on the Old Testament: The Minor Prophets* (Grand Rapids, MI: William Eerdmans Publishing Company, 1978), 10: 302.

9   Cited in the Internet source *www. Aish.Com* (February 9, 2003).

10   Pearl, op. cit., 181.

11   Rabbi Y.M. Tuchichinsky. "Ask the Rabbi," *Ohr Somayach International* (June 5, 1999), issue 239.

12   Ibid.

CHAPTER 4

CREMATION PAST AND PRESENT

What we call progress is the exchange
of one Nuisance for another Nuisance.
—Havelock Ellis

Although the methodology for cremating a deceased human in the distant past differed from the methodology of today, the end result was and is essentially the same. Both methods destroyed the body with fire, and both methods are still the most violent way to dispose of a human body. The discussion in the present chapter, however, focuses primarily on some of the material and nonmaterial effects of today's cremation and how they differ from cremation in the past, along with who now chooses to be cremated.

Cremation's Ancient Ways

To cremate a deceased human being in ancient times required erecting a stack of wood several feet high and somewhat longer and wider than the respective corpse. In the lower portion of the stack, tufts of grass or other less-dense materials were often wedged between the logs to help fuel the fire. The Romans, for instance, frequently had the wooden logs coated with pitch. Then the body was laid on the pyre, usually covered with fat derived from cattle specially slaughtered for this reason, particularly for high-social-status individuals. Frequently mourners would also cut off locks of hair and toss them on the burning corpse. It was common for the Romans to open the eyes of the corpse before submitting it to the flames so that the eyes could look to the heavens (Pliny, *Natural History* XI:150). And Cicero, the Roman philosopher and author (first century BC), notes even though his countrymen practiced cremation, they also performed the act of *os resectum*. This required cutting off a corpse's finger and burying it before cremation, apparently a ritual done in deference to the ancient practice of earth burial (Pliny, *De legibus* II:22, 55).

When the preparations for a cremation were completed, someone, commonly a member of the departed person's family, ignited the funeral pyre, or *rogus,* as the Romans called it. Near the end of the cremation process, as the flames diminished, next of kin often poured wine on the embers to extinguish them. Here it is interesting to note that the bones of the cremated body that for the most part did not burn (as noted in greater detail below), were either buried or placed in an urn or *ossarium* in Roman terminology. Many urns ranged from about twenty to twenty-four inches in height in order to accommodate the unburned thigh and leg bones, together with the ashes that resulted from the body's flesh and muscles.

Here it is fitting to note that bones are inorganic matter, and thus they, unlike the body's flesh, do not burn to ashes. Today, with modern furnaces that produce an optimum temperature ranging between 1500 and 1800 degrees Fahrenheit, the unburned bones come out in clumps of various sizes. They are then pulverized in a cremulator. These pulverized bones resemble dry fertilizer granules that are then combined with the body's ashes and placed into an urn considerably smaller than the ancient Roman urns.

In the days of the Roman cremation, unburned bones were sometimes crushed, as we learn from Lactantius (early church father, d. ca. 320). He writes that when the pagan Romans executed some Christians during the church's first three hundred years, they also sometimes despitefully cremated some and then crushed the unburned bones before they threw them into a river or a sea (*De Mortibus Persecutorum,* 21).

Since the human corpse in ancient times was commonly cremated on a stack of wood, the survivors could not entirely separate the body's ashes from the ashes of the wood, for the two were not always clearly distinguishable. Thus, some of the gathered ashes were a mixture of the corpse's ashes and ashes from the burned wood. The only remains that were positively those of the cremated body were the unburned bones that were usually placed into an urn or cast into a river. The latter is still done by Hindus, Sikhs, Buddhists, and other groups in India and in neighboring countries, where open-air cremations are still common.

Most Roman cremations took seven to eight hours to consume the corpse, plus another two hours for survivors to pick out the bone fragments interspersed among the ashes resulting from the body and the wood. Usually, the fire was lit at night and left to burn on its own, but often it had to be reignited the next morning.[1]

The Decline of Cremation in Ancient Rome

As already noted, the Romans, before and during the early years of Christianity, commonly cremated many of their dead, but they did not burn their infants, whom they usually buried. The poor, the indigent, undertakers, gladiators, slaves, and executed criminals were also treated differently. These culturally undesirables were usually not buried but left to birds of prey, dogs, and wolves or cast into the *puticuli* (open-air pits) located by Rome's Esquiline gate.[2]

By the mid-fourth century the burning of human corpses had essentially come to an end among the Romans, a phenomenon that some historians see the result of Christianity's influence. John Castleman Swinburne-Hanham (a British cremationist) credited Christianity with ending cremation in the Roman Empire. He wrote, "There can be little doubt that the practice of cremation in modern Europe was at first stopped, and since then prevented in great measure, by the Christian doctrine of the resurrection of the body."[3]

But some argue that the move away from cremation came too soon after Christianity was legalized in AD 313 for it to have prompted this major cultural change.[4] This argument, however, overlooks the fact that the Christian rejection of cremation was notably prominent in the empire long before Christianity was legalized. It can also be argued that it was not necessary for Christianity to have had legal status in order for it to have prompted this major cultural change. The contention that Christianity's opposition eventually led the Romans to abandon cremation gains some support in light of the strong criticism Caecilius, the Roman pagan, directed at Christians in about AD 195 for their spurning cremation. Angrily, he stated that Christians "execrate our funeral pyres and condemn cremation" (Minucius Felix, *Octavius* 11:4). It is not likely Caecilius would have voiced this indictment had Christianity's opposition to cremation been only a minor cultural irritation that had little or no effects.

Even though Roman cremation ended in the fourth century, it had not ended in all parts of Europe. As late as the eighth century some pagans in the hinterlands of Germania (Saxony) were still burning their dead. This lingering practice in some regions led Charlemagne the Great (ruler of the Holy Roman Empire from 754 to 814), influenced by Christianity, to outlaw cremation in 785. He made cremation a capital crime.[5]

Cremation Modernized

As noted in chapter 1, during the first half of the 1800s, some cremation advocates spoke at conferences, published articles and books, and even conducted some cremations, primarily in Europe, but also some in the United States. But it was not until 1874 (as noted earlier) that the quest for burning the dead in the West attained a permanent presence in England and the United States, in part the result of modernization. Previously, Prussia in 1855 had made the first formal effort to legalize cremation, but it did not succeed until 1911.[6] Following the initially failed efforts of the Prussian pro-cremationists in 1855, an international congress of medical experts met in Florence, Italy, in 1869, contending that earth burial was unhygienic. Four years later, the desire to cremate deceased humans received additional emphasis when Professor Lodovico Brunetti, from Italy's Padua University in 1873 at the Vienna Exposition showed cremation could effectively be accomplished by using gas or coal furnaces in place of pyres. He exhibited the cremated remains of one person in a glass container twelve inches long, eight inches wide, and eight inches deep. As already noted, bones as inorganic matter do not burn to ashes. The contents of Brunetti's cremated specimen weighed about three and three-quarter pounds.[7] Apparently he had crushed or pulverized the unburned bone fragments, similar to what is done in today's cremation process.

The cremation efforts of medical representatives at this international gathering in Vienna and Brunetti's advocacy spread almost immediately to England, where the cremation movement appealed "not only to atheists and freethinkers but also to Spiritualists and Theosophists, Unitarians, and Universalists."[8] Thus, as noted in chapter 1, Sir Henry Thompson in 1874 organized The Cremation Society of England. And in 1878, the newly formed Cremation Society of England built a crematory in Woking in Surrey. However, no cremations occurred in it until 1885, and then only as a result of a court decision. But a couple of private cremations had already taken place before the 1884 court decision.[9] The court's ruling was the result of William Price who, in conformity with his pagan-Druid beliefs, cremated his illegitimate son in January 1884 on a self-made funeral pyre on a hill on his own property.[10] (He had named his son Iesu Grist.) And in 1902, England's cremation advocates won another victory when the British Parliament passed the Cremation Act, legalizing it.

But even before these events, the first private crematory was built in the United States in 1876 in Washington, Pennsylvania. And it was also in 1876 that the first corpse, Baron de Palm (a devotee of Voltaire, the deistic critic of Christianity), was incinerated in this crematory. And in opposition to the long-standing, customary reading of biblical selections at funerals, Baron de Palm's friends at the committal ceremony selected readings from Charles Darwin and from some Hindu scriptures.[11] Although he was the first to be cremated in a crematory, his was not the first recorded cremation in the United States. In 1792, almost a hundred years before the formal push for cremation had begun in Europe and in America, Colonel Henry Laurens, who once served in George Washington's continental army and who feared bring buried alive (a real fear of many at that time), had himself cremated and his ashes scattered on his South Carolina estate. (No record seems to exist relative to what was done with his unburned bones, whether they had been pulverized or not.) In the 1870s, the promoting of cremation had spread to other countries as well. Germany, for instance, built its first crematory in Dresden, Saxony, in 1874 and another in Gotha in 1878.

Even though cremation reappeared in the West in the 1800s, popular acceptance did not happen until almost a hundred years later. For instance, before the 1960s cremation in the United States and in Canada was extremely rare. According to Stephen Prothero, it was not until 1963 that cremation began to attain relative acceptance in the United States.[12] Earlier, I documented this phenomenon in chapter 1, where the data show cremation rates began to increase notably in the mid-1960s, and from that time they continued their upward spiral during the next five decades, right to the present day.

The Body's Reaction

A crematory's furnace resembles a large oven and is called a "retort" in the funeral industry. After the body is placed into the retort, it is fired up, ranging between 1,500 and 1,800 degrees Fahrenheit for approximately two hours.[13] During the procedure a jet engine–like flame attacks the body. For an extremely obese person, it usually takes longer to consume the corpse. As the fire intensifies and consumes the dead body, a number of physiological reactions occur. Whether the cremation takes place on an open-air funeral pyre or in a modern crematory, the reactions of the body are similar. These reactions are not pleasant to describe, but given the growing popularity and increasing frequency of cremation in our society today, it would be less than candid not to note the body's reactions to the destructive flames. Moreover, in a free and open society, where people have the right to know so they can make informed decisions regarding matters affecting them or their loved ones, it only seems appropriate to report what transpires in the act of cremation. It can also be argued that if individuals really knew what takes place in the cremation process, it might prompt many (especially Christians) to rethink the advisability of having themselves, a spouse, a child, or a relative cremated someday. For much of the recent increase in cremation rates appears to be the result of many people blindly conforming to their secularized culture's values, often without having given it any serious thought, and about which they have acquired little or no reliable information. Here is how a physician and anatomist describes a typical cremation.

> The coffin is introduced into the furnace where it rapidly catches fire, bulges and wraps, and the coffin sides may collapse and fall, exposing the remains to the direct effect of the flames. The skin and hair at once scorch, char and burn ... The muscles slowly contract, and there may be a steady spreading of the thighs with gradually developing flexion of the limbs ... Occasionally there is swelling of the abdomen before the skin and abdominal muscles

char and split ... Destruction of the soft tissues gradually exposes parts of the skeleton. The skull is soon devoid of covering, then the bones of limbs appear, commencing at the extremities of the limbs where they are relatively poorly covered by muscles or fat, and the ribs also become exposed. The small bones of the fingers, wrists and ankles remain united by their ligaments for a surprising length of time, maintaining their anatomical relationships even though the hands and feet fall away from the adjacent long bones. The abdominal contents burn slowly, and the lungs more slowly still ... The brain is especially resistant to complete combustion ... Eventually the spine becomes visible as the viscera disappear, and the bones glow whitely [sic] in the flames, and the skeleton falls apart.[14]

Being aware of what transpires in the process of cremation, as just described, one observer uttered the following, sobering words. "To a person of refined Christian culture it must be most repulsive to think of a friend being treated like a beef roast in an oven, with all its running fats and sizzling tissues."[15] Some other critics, knowing what takes place in the act of cremation, say they would not subject their dead dog to this kind of violent destruction.

Cremated Remains: Not What Many Think

It is commonly and widely believed that after the human corpse has been burned, only ashes are left, regardless of whether the cremation occurs on an open-air funeral pyre or in the furnace of a modern crematory. This is a mistaken conclusion, one that has largely been perpetuated by our society's use of the word ashes because it fails to note that the remains of a cremated body are not just ashes. The bones of the body (as previously indicated) do not burn, for their content is about sixty percent inorganic and thus noncombustible matter.[16]

The ancient Greek poet Homer (eighth or ninth century BC) notes after Hector's body had been cremated "brethren and his comrades gathered the white bones" (*Iliad* 24:793). Similarly, the Latin poet Virgil mentions that after a body was cremated the bones were placed into urns (*Aeneid* 6:219–29). In the Old Testament we read that when King Saul and his three sons were cremated, the men of Jabesh-gilead took their unburned bones and buried them under the tamarisk tree at Jabesh (1 Samuel 31:13). And when Roman dignitaries were cremated, their bones were commonly gathered and then survivors cleansed them with wine and milk.[17]

If the bones of cremated corpses do not burn, then why do modern urns not contain any unburned bones? The answer is simple. The unburned bones, as mentioned earlier, are pulverized in today's crematories by a grinding-up process that reduces the bones to small granules.[18] These pulverized remains are not just ashes, even though people like to refer to them as such.

There is another detail that the public does not really know about cremated ashes, namely, that sometimes a white-colored substance is added to make them look more attractive.[19] Many not only want a deceased person to look nice lying in a casket, but those who choose cremation also want the ashes to look appealing.

Since the bones of cremated corpses today are mechanically ground up and then mixed with the ashes from the nonbone parts of the body, the entire contents of an urn, depending on the size of the corpse, ordinarily weigh "between four and eight pounds."[20] Thus, today's urns are substantially smaller than the urns of the Roman era when the unburned bones were usually not crushed.

This difference cannot be ignored. In the past, when the unburned bones were commonly placed into an urn tall enough to accommodate them, the cremated bodies still had something in common with the bones of bodies lying in a grave or in an ossuary, but today's cremated bodies have really nothing in common with cremations of by-gone years. This difference makes present-day cremations far more radical.

Housing and Disposing of the Ashes

The ashes of cremated corpses have in recent years presented new business opportunities. Numerous businesses, especially within the last decade, have become engaged in producing and marketing various items from the remains of cremated individuals. The following are some current examples.

A Variety of Urns

As might be imagined in an affluent society such as the United States and Canada, individuals who incinerate their relatives or friends can select from a large number of urns. They come in all colors, shapes, and designs. They are available in the form of Japanese pagodas, Egyptian temples, closed books, and open books, and some are even modeled resembling golf bags. Some are made of marble, bronze or wood; others are biodegradable, made to please those who are environmentally conscious. And as might also be imagined, many urns are expensive, selling in the vicinity of $2,000 or more.

Ashes in Stained-Glass Windows

People are not necessarily limited to urns, for at least one place, namely, Robert H. Schuller's Crystal Cathedral in Garden Grove, California, has had the ashes of some individuals crafted into its stained glass windows. This building is now owned by the Roman Catholic Church.

Jewelry from Ashes

All sorts of jewelry items with pendants displaying hearts, personal initials, tear drops, gemstones, and even Christian crosses are now available. These items use the ashes in two ways. Some pendants, for instance, have hollowed-out cavities filled with a cremated person's ashes and then sealed. Some jewelry items are also made from a cremated person's carbon. The finished product resembles shiny gemstones. Some are made in the United States, and others are produced in foreign countries, for instance, China and India. And interestingly, a human corpse can yield up to fifty jewelry stones of varying sizes, more than most survivors desire to have. Thus, most of the cremated person's ashes are not used for producing jewelry items. This still requires survivors to dispose of the remainder in some other manner, frequently by scattering them at some location.

Vinyl Records from Ashes

Recently, the creative ingenuity of cremation businesses has found another use for dead people's ashes. A British company now offers vinyl-audio records made from cremated ashes. The records are made by using vinyl pellets from a corpse's ashes. This amalgam is then pressed into vinyl discs on which given audible sounds are recorded. Customers may pick any audio they want with the proviso that the company is not responsible for any copyright infringements.[21]

Ashes Shot into Space

In addition to making cremated ashes into jewelry or vinyl records, some survivors have opted for more unconventional means to dispose of their relative's incinerated remains. For instance, Timothy Leary, the LSD guru of the 1960s, had his ashes blasted into space by a Spanish satellite in April 1997, and the ashes of Gene Roddenberry, creator of

Star Trek, accompanied those of Leary. And on July 31, 1999, Eugene Shoemaker, a NASA geologist who died in an automobile accident, had his ashes rocketed to the moon. One firm in California takes survivors of the deceased on an airplane, permitting them to jettison their cremated relative onto the Pacific Ocean, and sometimes, as this is done, the Lord's Prayer is spoken or Psalm 23 is read.[22] California has a company (Pacific Memorials in Los Angeles) that mixes a cremated person's ashes with gun powder and then packs both of them in fireworks; an Iowa firm (Canuck's Sportsman's Memorials in Des Moines) will upon request put the ashes into shotgun shells for the sports-minded hunting friends or relatives of the deceased person.[23] In Alabama, a firm named Holy Smoke loads ashes into shotgun shells and rifle cartridges. And a son of a Lutheran pastor of the liberal Evangelical Lutheran Church in America (ELCA) in Marine on St. Croix, Minnesota, shot his father's cremated remains into the sky in a fireworks display on July 4, 2005. In keeping with many cremationists who deny the future resurrection of the body, he said, "We don't believe in the literal resurrection of the body."[24] Whom he meant by "we," he did not say. His statement, of course, runs counter to the New Testament's teaching regarding the bodily resurrection and also counter to the Apostles' Creed and the Nicene Creed.

Scattering the Ashes

As is well-known, the so-called ashes are often scattered or "strewn," as the Church of England euphemistically calls it. It is estimated in England that about 90 percent of the ashes are scattered at various locations. In the United States the scattering of the ashes is less common, with about 25 percent being disposed of in this way.[25] Although the Roman Catholic Church does not officially approve of scattering ashes, it is nevertheless done by some Catholics. For instance, the family of John Kennedy Jr., members of the Roman Catholic church, did so. Young Kennedy was killed in private plane crash in July 1999.

The family had him cremated, and his ashes were cast from a yacht onto the waters of the Atlantic Ocean, an act that some in the media, still accustomed to earth-burial language, called "buried at sea."

Tubes for Scattering

Since the end of the 1990s, the funeral industry, in its promotion of cremation, has been marketing scattering tubes. They are tube-like containers that range from about six to twelve inches in height and about three to five inches in diameter. Some have perforated lids to facilitate the scattering process and are decorated with various colorful designs. Most are biodegradable and are advertised as giving dignity to the scattering of a person's remains.

Scattering Ashes Conveys a Message

Regardless of the euphonic terms that are given to scattering a cremated person's ashes, the observation by the French scholar Philippe Aries is worth noting, especially by Christians. According to him, scattering ashes reveals a "desire to break with the Christian tradition."[26] This assessment by Aries is evidently not known or ignored by Christians who opt for cremation and then have a relative or friend scatter the person's burned remains.

There is a certain irony in the scattering of ashes, given that at one time (mid 1800s in Europe) only the ashes of cremated criminals were scattered in order to show the severity of their crime.[27] There is still another irony. It pertains to the origin of scattering a cremated person's ashes. According to Viscount de Chateaubriand, it was first conceived by "impious miscreants ... in order to destroy the memory of the past [and] it was tantamount to a conspiracy to overturn the world."[28]

In the United States, laws vary as to what may be done with the ashes. Not all states permit survivors to scatter them on open property. Moreover, the scattering is usually not permitted in state parks, beaches, or city parks. On the other hand, survivors do sometimes scatter the ashes on sites where it is not permitted. Given that ashes are essentially invisible after they are dispersed in the grass, some individuals scatter them when no one sees the scattering taking place, and thus some sites that ban the scattering of ashes may have them unknowingly.

Shipping the Ashes

In addition to how the ashes might be disposed of, there are other problems associated with them. Unknown to the general public, and to the bereaved of a cremated person, ashes are sometimes shipped in cardboard boxes that have been known to develop breaks and thus lose some or much of their content.[29] As a result of such leakages, United Parcel Service (UPS) and FedEx now refuse to transport the ashes of any cremated human body.

Ashes, Plus What?

It has been reported that partially filled containers are sometimes unethically filled up with ashes from fireplaces, unknown to the survivors.[30] Partially filled boxes are not the only problem that can be encountered. For example, sometimes when survivors scatter the ashes of a loved one, they may find denture pieces from someone else's ashes.[31] Experiences such as these indicate the ashes that people sometimes receive may not be from the assumed person, or they may also be mixed with ashes from some other individual(s). Moreover, even when no unethical act of cremation takes place, it is highly probable that least a small amount of ashes from some other cremated person will be present in the urn.[32] Furnaces (retorts) are not scrupulously scoured between cremations. Morticians only use a brush to sweep the ashes into a container before placing them in an urn. And interestingly, given that crematories are not well regulated in many American states,[33] multiple cremations can and sometimes do occur at the same time, as happened in 1989 in Los Angeles, California.[34] Thus, recipients sometimes do not know what portion of the ashes they have on hand is really from their cremated relative, and what portion is from someone else.

There is still another problem. Sometimes family members do not know whether the ashes they have received are really those of their deceased relative or whether they are ashes from wood or from some other formerly combustible material. The American public became aware of this kind of deception in February 2002 when it heard about scores of human bodies that were supposedly cremated but were found lying in the woods near Noble, Georgia, where the crematory operator had discarded them. Because it is relatively easy to deceive people with ashes from wood, or ashes from some other product, one family of a deceased person in Georgia had received ashes from wood chips mixed with regular cement. And more recently a university in Florida had allegedly obtained dead bodies without authorization for its mortuary studies program. These bodies were to have been cremated but were used instead to teach mortuary students embalming techniques.[35] Hence, in this instance, what kind of ashes had the relatives or friends of the deceased received?

Consequences of Scattering Ashes

The ashes of some cremated humans are not scattered but placed in mausoleums, columbaria, and sometimes even buried in cemeteries. But in many countries this practice is becoming virtually extinct. For instance, as noted above, in England the ashes of the vast majority of the cremated dead are scattered. In Japan, where the scattering of ashes traditionally was not practiced, it is now becoming more common. Thus, with the growing practice of scattering ashes, there is no longer any consecrated ground or place for countless departed individuals, as once was true for centuries with earth burials in cemeteries, where survivors can visit the grave to honor and remember their departed relative or friend.

Visits to the cemetery reminded the surviving family members of the brevity and uncertainty of their own lives and that someday they too would have to leave this world to meet their Maker. For Christians visiting a cemetery was also a reminder that someday all who are in their graves, as Christ said, "will hear his voice and come out" (John 5:28).

Finally, given that many survivors of a cremated person are now increasingly scattering his or her ashes brings to mind the words of a concerned Christian clergyman and also a funeral director. Treating the deceased body in this manner, he contends, "is an affront to the resurrection; it is an action that proclaims, 'Good luck trying to raise up this scattered and destroyed body.'"[36]

Cremation Is Not "Green"

Advocates and promoters of cremation often argue that graves in cemeteries pollute, and therefore society should encourage people to opt for cremation, which is touted as pollution-free. At first blush this argument sounds plausible, but does it square with the facts? No, not really. Research shows that crematories emit relatively high levels of dioxins and trace metals from the incinerated bodies and in some instances from the caskets that are often part of the cremation process. Mercury is emitted into the air from the deceased individual's teeth fillings, and if the person had been fitted with a plutonium-powered pacemaker, radioactivity is released into the air.[37] One study reported, "The increasing use of cremation could lead to problems in view of the thermal instability of mercury alloys, the volatility of the free metal, its cumulative toxicity, and the aggregate amounts now involved."[38] In addition, the incineration of obese bodies sends heavy black smoke into the atmosphere.[39] As one observer has noted,

"A plume of black acrid smoke rises from the ill-disguised chimney, bearing its load of burnt plastic and terylene up, up and away, to make its contribution to the 'greenhouse effect.' Cremation may be 'clean' but it's certainly not 'green.'"[40]

According to the Cremation Association of North America (CANA), the following emissions occur when a corpse is incinerated: particulate matter, carbon monoxide, nitrogen oxides, sulfur dioxide, hydrogen chloride, metals (mercury, cadmium, lead), dioxins and furans.[41] Most of these "pollutants increased when the operating temperature was raised."[42]

In 2012, a study examined the emissions from a crematory in Santa Cruz, California. It found the level of mercury exposure from a crematory was twenty-two times more than the acceptable air standard.[43] And interestingly, the *Santa Cruz Sentinel* reported that there are no federal or state standards for mercury emissions.[44] Moreover, overseas in the United Kingdom it is predicted that by 2020 crematoria will be the largest single contributor to airborne mercury emissions.[45] Thus, cremating human bodies is not as "green" as many erroneously assume.

Conclusion

In spite of modern technology, cremating the dead today still has some similarities to open-air pyres of the past. First, both methods are still the most violent, destructive way to dispose of the human body. Second, in both processes the bones, as inorganic material, still do not burn, despite the extremely intense and concentrated heat of modern furnaces. Thus, compared to open-air funeral pyres, today's cremating differs somewhat, primarily in regard to what is done with the unburned bones. Today's crematories pulverize the unburned bones and then mix the pulverized result with the ashes that are the product of the body's softer, nonbone content.

Apart from the methodology, the biggest change that has occurred in cremation since it was brought back to the West, so to speak, from pagan Rome pertains to who is now cremated. When cremation first reappeared in the mid-1800s, it was primarily promoted and practiced by agnostics, atheists, Universalists, and antichurch individuals. They largely opted for cremation as an act of psychological, religious rebellion. Today, with more and more Christians choosing cremation, the line between Christians and many irreligious or antireligious cremationists has largely been erased. This phenomenon is further discussed in chapter 7.

[1] David Noy, "Half-Burnt On An Emergency Pyre: Roman Cremations Which Went Wrong," *Greece and Rome* (October, 2000), 187.

[2] Harold Whetstone Johnstone, *The Private Life of the Romans* (Chicago: Scott, Foresman & Company, 1905), 317–18.

[3] John Castleman Swinburne-Hanham, "Cremation," *The Encyclopaedia Britannica* (Cambridge, England: At the University Press, 1910), 7:403.

[4] A.D. Nock, "Cremation and Burial in the Roman Empire," *Harvard Theological Review* (October, 1932), 326.

[5] M. B. Walsh, "Cremation (Moral Aspects)," *The New Catholic Encyclopedia* (San Francisco, CA: McGraw-Hill and Company, 1967), 4:440.

[6] Paul E. Irion, *Cremation* (Philadelphia, PA: Fortress Press, 1968), 19.

[7] Sir Henry Thompson, "The Treatment of Body after Death," *The Contemporary Review* (January, 1874), 327.

[8] Prothero, op. cit., 137.

[9] Florence G. Findel, *Cremation* (London: Williams and Norgate Limited, 1930), 20-21.

[10] Hugo Erichsen, *The Cremation of the Dead* (Detroit, MI: D.O. Haynes and Company, 1887), 59.

[11] Timothy George, "Cremation Confusion," *Christianity Today* (May 21, 2002), 66.

[12] Stephen Prothero, *Purified by Fire* (Berkeley, CA: University of California Press, 2001), 163.

[13] Phipps, op. cit., 33.

[14] W.E.D. Evans, *The Chemistry of Death* (Springfield, IL: Charles C. Thomas Publishers, 1963), 84-85.

15 James W. Fraser, *Cremation: Is It Christian?* (Neptune, NJ: Loizeaux Brothers, 1965), 11.

16 Kenneth V. Iserson, *Death to Dust: What Happens to the Dead Bodies* (Tucson, AZ: Galen Press, 1994), 236.

17 T.G. Tucker, *Life in the Roman World of Nero and St. Paul* (New York: The Macmillan Company, 1929), 445.

18 Phipps, op. cit., 33.

19 Iserson, op. cit., 264.

20 Ibid., 236.

21 "Recording Oldies," *World* (August 24, 2013), 18.

22 Prothero, op. cit., 203.

23 Flanagan, op. cit., 324.

24 "Memorial: Out with a Bang and Blaze," *GrandForksHerald.Com* (accessed July 12, 2005).

25 Anonymous, "Hot, Hot, Hot," *Forbes* (Winter, 1997), 50.

26 Philippe Aries, *Western Attitudes Towards Death From the Middle Ages to the Present* (Baltimore, MD: John Hopkins University Press, 1974), 91.

27 Viscount de Chateaubriand, *The Genius of Christianity*, trans. Charles L White (Baltimore, MD: John Murphy and Company, 1864), 517.

28 Ibid., 521.

29 Iserson, op. cit., 267.

30 Ibid.

31 Ibid., 265.

32 Ibid.

33 Kit R. Roane, "Burial Plots," *U.S. News and World Report* (March 11, 2002), 24.

34 John Johnson, "Macabre Tale of Scandal Rocks Cremation Industry," *Journal-Gazette* (Fort Wayne, IN, 1989), 9A.

35 "Conspiracy or Negligence?" *Mortuary Management* (December, 2002), 22.

36 Nathan Corl Minnich, "The Death of the Funeral," *Lutheran Forum Letter* (January, 2015), 3.

37 Iserson, op. cit., 554. Reportedly, these devices are now removed from the corpse before cremation takes place.

38 Allan Mills, "Mercury and Crematorium Chimneys," *Nature* (August 16, 1990), 615.

39 Iserson, op. cit., 262.

40 Julian Litten, *The English Way of Death: The Common Funeral Since 1450* (London: Robert Hale, 1991), 3.

41 "Emissions Testing Results," *Cremation Association of North America Website* (January 23, 2003), 1.

42 Ibid., 2.

43 "Mercury Emissions from California Crematory Halts Project," *Santa Cruz Sentinel* (August 2, 2012).

44 Ibid.

45 "Mercury and Its Uses/Emissions," www.zeromercury.org/index. php?options=com_content&view=article&id=211&Itemid=99 (accessed September 23, 2012).

CHAPTER 5

FROM CREMATING TO COMPOSTING

To innovate is not to reform.
—Edmund Burke

The rapid rise of cremation rates since the 1960s is getting the attention of many individuals and not just the so-called greenies but also many who are concerned about the pollution cremation produces. The fire-driven method of cremation furnaces (retorts) are a major source of air pollution, as documented in the preceding chapter. Many individuals want a more environmentally friendly method for disposing of deceased human beings. Thus, recently two new methods designed to dispose of human bodies are making their entry into the funeral business, and both seek to replace cremation as it is known and practiced today. Neither of these new methods uses fire to dispose of human corpses. One method is known as resomation, and it is already in operation in a number of locations. The other method, known as promession, may soon be operating as well.

Resomation

In 2007, Sandy Sullivan in Glasgow, Scotland, invented the resomation process by constructing a machine that disposes of dead humans by using a highly accelerated chemical process known as alkaline hydrolysis. In order to market his invention, Sullivan formed a commercial company, Resomation Limited. Although it is a European enterprise, the firm works closely with the Mayo Clinic in Minnesota that has since 2006 used a process quite similar to Sullivan's in its disposing of donated cadavers and amputated body parts.[1] It has also been used for the disposition of animal carcasses.

The word *resomation* is derived from the Greek word *resoma,* meaning rebirth or remaking of a body. But to use the word *resoma* for this method is somewhat disingenuous, for the dead person is not reborn or remade by this process but rather destroyed. The human corpse is usually wrapped in a bio-degradable shroud, sometimes made of silk, and then submerged in a solution of alkaline hydrolysis that ordinarily consists of about eighty gallons of water (depending on the size of the body) and about four gallons of potassium hydroxide, housed in a stainless-steel chamber. Given that potassium hydroxide (lye) is a key element in resomation, some critics have facetiously spoken of it as a corpse "coming through the lye."

The alkaline hydrolysis solution is pressurized and heated to about 180 degrees Celsius (350 degrees Fahrenheit) for about two to three hours. The process dissolves the body and leaves a small amount of leftover liquid that is greenish-brown, containing peptides, sugars, salts, amino acids, and soapy material from the person's body fat. This liquid is then drained into the municipal sewage system, or a committed environmentalist may take the liquid home and use it to fertilize his or her garden, namely using the resomated grandpa or grandma as fertilizer. After the liquid is taken out of the stainless chamber, the bone portions remain in the resomator, as the unit is called. The remaining bone portions are white, soft, porous, and crumbly. Next, they are dried under a heat lamp and then placed into a "cremulator" that pulverizes them into a powder that has the appearance of white flour. This white powder can be placed in an urn, similar to the pulverized contents of a regularly cremated body.

The average adult body yields approximately five to seven pounds of white powder.

Resomation is promoted as the "green way" to dispose of deceased bodies. Its promoters say it reduces the carbon footprint by 75 percent, as surgery components and teeth amalgams are physically removed, whereas in cremation the mercury in dental fillings vaporize and enter the atmosphere, polluting the air people breathe. Compared to cremation, resomation uses 85 percent less energy, and it emits one-third less greenhouse gases than cremation. Its advocates also say it appears less violent to survivors who are having a body disposed of without burning it in flames.

Many advocates of resomation, including some news reporters, call resomation "green cremation" or "bio-cremation,"[2] and sometimes it is also referred to as "water resolution" or "cryomation." Given that resomation is not currently well-known, adding the prefix *bio* to the familiar word *cremation* may make the process more appealing to environmentally minded individuals, and thus it may help market this new method for disposing of deceased human bodies.

In 2008, the Cremation Society of Great Britain formally decided to amend its charter to allow its members to choose resomation to dispose of their human bodies. This action by the Cremation Society helped give Sullivan's firm (Resomation Limited) national recognition and also needed social legitimation. Thus, in 2010, Resomation Limited received the prestigious British John Logie Baird Award. This award, interestingly, told the public that Sullivan's invention had much in common with what John Logie Baird (1888–1946), "The Father of Television," had accomplished.

The first "resomator" in the United States was installed in Columbus, Ohio, in 2011. But given that this process had not been legalized by Ohio's state legislature, the state ordered the funeral director to shut down his resomator.[3] However, about the time Ohio shut down the resomator in Columbus, a well-established funeral home in St. Petersburg, Florida, installed one in the summer of

2012. Then, in June 2012, a morturary in Stillwater, Minnesota, also installed a resomator. By August 2012, at least eight other American states had legalized the resomation process. Mortuaries outside of the United States have also recently installed resomators. In 2010, Eco Memorial Park in Stapylton, Queensland, Australia, chose to do so as well.[4] And in November 2012, Saskatchewan became the first Canadian province to approve and adopt the resomation process.

The funeral home that operates the resomator in Stillwater, Minnesota, resomated about 270 bodies in its first year of operation in 2012. The facility in St. Petersburg, Florida, resomated about 150 bodies in its first year (2012) of operation.[5] These two funeral homes, according to my contacts with them, try not to exceed the costs of a conventional cremation. The resomator costs about $400,000, and presently (2013) resomating a human body costs approximately $3,500. The St. Petersburg facility says it charges about a hundred dollars more than for a cremation.

Although resomation employs an entirely different process than regular cremation, it has the full support of the Cremation Association of North America (CANA). Organized in 1913, CANA is headquartered in Chicago, Illinois. Since its founding, CANA has been a strong advocate of cremation and other nonburial methods that dispose of human bodies.

In recent years, Roman Catholic bishops in the United States have opposed the acceptance of resomation when legislative bills were introduced to legalize it in given states. Whether the bishops will continue to oppose it remains to be seen. They may, however, eventually accept it, similar to Pope Paul VI having accepted cremation for Roman Catholics in 1963, even though the Holy See had formally condemned cremation several times in the 1880s and again in 1926.

Promession (Composting)

In 1999, ecologically minded Susanne Wiigh-Masak, a biologist, in Sweden invented the promator, the device of a promatorium. It is designed to dispose of a human corpse by promession, as its inventor calls it. The name *promession* is derived from the Italian *promessa,* meaning promise. Thus, this method promises the public that by disposing of the human corpse in this manner it converts the body into compost-like material, reputedly a positive environmental outcome, free of toxic air pollution emitted in the conventional cremation process.

The first step in promession places the body into a steel chamber, where it is slowly frozen for about ten days at minus eighteen degrees Celsius (zero degrees Fahrenheit). After the body is thoroughly frozen, it advances on a moving platform within a stainless steel sealed unit called a promator. Next the body is immersed in liquid nitrogen, where it encounters an intensely frigid temperature of minus 196 degrees Celsius (minus 320 Fahrenheit) for about two hours. This makes the corpse extremely brittle. Then it is placed into a vibrator, where sound waves pulverize it into a powder. The pulverized contents, however, still contain most of the body's water, thus requiring it to be dehydrated in a vacuum chamber from which the water evaporates into the atmosphere as natural steam, reputed to be harmless. This process reduces the human body's final weight by about 70 percent. After this step, mercury, surgical parts, and other metals present are separated and removed by a magnetic technique, leaving about twenty-five to thirty kilograms (fifty-five to sixty-five pounds) of dry powder that is placed into a biodegradable casket, usually made from corn starch. The powdered remains (called "promains") are then buried relatively shallow in a biodegradable casket in some upper-mulch-forming layers of the soil where microorganisms turn the casket and its contents into humus (compost) in approximately six to twelve months.

Critics argue that promession nullifies all respect for the human body because it reduces the body to compost that is often used to nourish plant life. This criticism is not unwarranted, for Susanne Wiigh-Masak, the inventor of promession, has admitted, "The remains make splendid potting soil."[6] Thus, this end product of a human body is a noteworthy departure from what the Bible says about the human body's ultimate remains. Genesis 3:19 states, "For dust you are, and to dust you shall remain." It says nothing about the body's final remains becoming something other than dust. Promession's so-called "potting soil" is not dust. In addition to promession, conventional cremation also departs from the description in Genesis 3:19 when its advocates say cremated ashes are similar to dust. This is false, for Genesis 3:19 says nothing about deceased bodies turning to ashes. It only talks about the body returning to its original state from which God created it, namely, from dust. And it needs to be underscored the Bible also nowhere states the human corpse will ever turn to ashes.

This new method of disposing human bodies has received verbal support from a number of entities. The Association of Parishes within the Lutheran Church of Sweden published a booklet in 2003 that provided positive information concerning promession. Susanne Wiigh-Masak named her company Promessa Organic Burial AB, and by mid-2011 she reportedly had received inquiries from more than sixty countries. But to date these countries have not purchased this new invention, and so her method has thus far not been used for the disposing of human beings.

Conclusion

Given we are currently living in an era where increasing emphasis is placed on being environmentally conscious and responsible, complemented by behavior that endeavors to correct past environmental practices, it is not surprising that the conventional method of cremation is being questioned by environmentally minded individuals whose goal is to replace it with a method they think is better for the environment. But whether that goal will be achieved remains to be seen, for the two new methods, resomation and promession, are still largely unknown to the public. That the names of both methods are entirely new to the English language is not helpful either. To cope with the latter problem, promoters of the two methods are now calling the process "biocremation." Clearly, this is intended to get people to see and accept the new methods as being similar to cremation, which so many in the Western world have already accepted. But whether the term biocremation will become more common and get people to accept these two methods remains to be seen.

Finally, these two new ways of disposing of deceased humans are equally incompatible with the biblical, theological concerns the early Christians had when they rejected the cremation practices of the ancient Romans who burned the body either on a pyre of wood or in a hollowed-out pit.

---

1   "Bio-cremation (Resomation)," www.mayoclinic.org/body-donation/ resomation.html (accessed October 9, 2012).

2   The term biocremation is a misnomer used by some, evidently to appeal to individuals who have accepted cremation. Resomation dissolves the body chemically. It does not use flames or intense heat to dispose of the body.

3   *The Columbus Dispatch* (March 23, 2011).

4   Marina Kameny (*Time News Service,* September 28, 2010).

5   I obtained these statistics from the St. Petersburg, Florida, mortuary facility and from the other one in Stillwater, Minnesota, by telephone.

6   "Pagan Dying and Death Options" (http://paganpastoraloutreach.ca/death/ news.htm), accessed January 30, 2006.

CHAPTER 6

THE EARLY CHRISTIANS REJECTED CREMATION

You can judge the quality of their faith by the way they behave.
—Tertullian

There is a well-known saying, "When in Rome, do as the Romans do." However, when the first Christians came from the Holy Land (Palestine) and settled in and around the city of Rome, they did not imitate the Romans. One notable example was their firm, stalwart rejection of Rome's long-standing custom of cremating their dead.

Christians as Exiles (*Paroikoi*)

Although the early Christians lived and interacted with pagan Romans, they notably distinguished themselves in a number of ways. Foremost, they saw themselves as *paroikoi* (exiles), a term the apostle Peter used in 1 Peter 2:11, where he told Christians they were "sojourners and exiles [*paroikoi*]." As *paroikoi*, they heeded St. Paul's admonition. "Do not be conformed to this world, but be transformed by the renewal of your mind, that by testing you may discern what is the will of God, what is good and acceptable and perfect" (Romans 12:2). This meant they refused to call the Roman emperor "Lord"; they declined to drop a few harmless-looking drops of olive oil on statues of pagan deities or on altars; they did not attend Roman games, theatrical shows, or gladiatorial contests; they condemned abortion, child abandonment, infanticide, and suicide; they also rejected homosexuality and shunned promiscuous heterosexual behavior; and they consistently opposed and rejected cremation. Their refusing to participate in these long-standing pagan practices frequently resulted in their being hated and sometimes persecuted; sometimes some were enslaved, imprisoned, or tortured, and sometimes some were even executed (martyred). Some of the latter were at times spitefully cremated, according to the fourth-century church father Lactantius (*De Mortibus Persecutorum*, 21).

Church historians have often noted that the early Christians, vis-à-vis the pagans, were known for loving one another. But long before historians called attention to the first Christians loving one another, Tertullian (Latin church father, late second century) quoted the Romans. "Look how they love one another" (*Apologeticum* 39:7). In citing this description, historians have failed to note why the Christians loved one another, namely, because they saw themselves as *paroikoi*.[1] It was an important self-concept for them; it functioned as a social bond, a bond that helped them endure the social ridicule and persecutions they experienced for three hundred years. Will Durant, the renowned historian, once said, "The early Christians were a reproving example to the pagan world."[2] Their reproving Rome's pagan practice of cremation, for example, was part of their status as *paroikoi*.

Why Christians Rejected Cremation

When the Christians in the second half of the first century came to Rome and its surrounding areas, they found that the pagan Romans for the most part disposed many of their dead by cremating them. Coming from Palestine, where they and their Jewish ancestors had always buried their dead, cremation was a cultural and a theological shock. Thus, the early Christians stalwartly and consistently opposed and rejected Rome's longstanding, pagan practice of cremating the dead. And they did so for several reasons.

They Desired Burial Similar to Jesus

Given that Jesus, right after his crucifixion, was buried or laid in Arimathea's tomb, the early Christians also desired to be buried or entombed in God's good earth. It was another way of their wanting to follow Jesus, not just while they were alive but also when their earthly sojourn had come to an end. Alfred C. Rush in his book *Death and Burial in Christian Antiquity* (1949) says for the early Christians, "A very powerful motive for earth burial was the burial of Christ himself."[3] And as with Christ, all were buried without embalmment.

They Had Biblical Precedents for Earth Burial

Before the Christians migrated to Rome as *paroikoi*, they knew of countless predecessors who, in the Old Testament era, were buried or entombed. They also had noteworthy examples of individuals in the New Testament who were buried in graves. For instance, Acts 8:2 states, "Devout men buried Stephen." He became the first Christian martyr, stoned to death in Jerusalem in the nascent years of Christianity. John the Baptist, whom Herod Antipas had decapitated, was buried by his disciples (Matthew 14:12). Not a single person whose death is noted in the New Testament was disposed of in any other manner than by inhumation. Even Ananias and Sapphira, who were struck dead for lying to the Holy Spirit, were interred (Acts 5:3–10).

Given the biblical tradition of earth burial among the early Christians, the French historian Henri Daniel-Rops has said that among the Christians "there never was any question of cremating the dead."[4] They had no other desire than what was done with their biblical predecessors. Thus, what the pagans did with the bodies of their deceased by cremating them was unthinkable and repugnant to them.

The Christians also had support for earth burial from what Jesus once stated. "Leave the dead to bury their own dead" (Luke 9:60). Although these words primarily chided the man who said he first needed to bury his deceased father before he could follow Jesus, they also indicate Jesus accepted the Jewish practice of earth burial. Here it is appropriate to remember the words of two modern critics of cremation. "Jesus attacked many Jewish traditions, but burial of the dead was not one of them."[5] Note also, Jesus did not say, "Let the dead cremate their dead." Had he said the latter, his words not only would have been an affront to this man of the Hebrew culture, but they would also have been in conflict with what Jesus once said, namely, that at his second coming all who are in their graves "will hear his voice and come out" (John 5:29).

They Believed in the Sanctity of the Human Body

It is well known among church historians that the early Christians strongly opposed infanticide, child abandonment, abortion, and suicide because they believed in the sanctity of the human body. In their minds, the sanctity of the human body did not come to an end when a person died. They saw the human being as the crown of God's creation, for according to Genesis 1:27, man was made in the image of God, and although that image was tarnished by man's fall into sin, they sincerely believed the words of the Psalmist. "You have made him [man] a little lower than the heavenly beings and crowned him with glory and honor" (Psalm 8:5). In addition, St. Paul told the Christians in Corinth, "Do you not know that you are God's temple and that God's Spirit dwells in you?" (1 Corinthians 3:16). And in the same verse he added, "If anyone destroys God's temple, God will destroy him."

In light of these words by Paul, did the early Christians believe God would destroy them if they practiced cremation? It cannot be documented that they did, but it is quite possible and certainly not implausible that these words contributed to their unfailing anticremation posture. Moreover, Paul reminded them three chapters later, "You are not your own, for you were bought with a price. So glorify God in your body" (1 Corinthians 6:19–20). In short, as Christians, their bodies were not only the temple of the Holy Spirit, but their bodies were also not their own; they belonged to God, and thus they were to glorify him with their bodies. However, they could not envision how cremating their bodies could possibly glorify God.

So, did the early Christians think they were glorifying God by not cremating their bodies? Again, we do not know from any recorded evidence that Paul's words helped motivate them to reject cremation, but that possibility cannot be ruled out. For as H. Richard Rutherford has stated, "Historically, Christians have always devoted great attention to the body of the deceased, honoring it as a temple of the Holy Spirit."[6]

In regard to a Christian's body being the temple of the Holy Spirit, one historian summed up the effect of Paul's words this way: "The will of God, they [the Christians] believed, pointed to burial, which was Christ's mode, and a more loving and reverent rite. The body was the instrument of the soul and the temple of the Holy Spirit, and must be reverenced accordingly."[7] In a similar vein, the church father Origen (185-254) defended the burying of persons because cremating the body showed no respect for the body that once housed its soul (*Against Celsus* 5:24). Thus, concerned Christians saw cremation not only as disrespectful of the human body but also as an ungodly act.

The high value Christians ascribed to the human body, whether alive or dead, in part also reflected their Judaic heritage. One of the most unnerving thoughts a Hebrew in the Old Testament could experience was to imagine that his or her dead body would someday be left for animals or birds to devour. Here it is fitting to recall the words David said to Goliath. "I strike you down and cut off your head. And I will give the dead bodies of the host of the Philistines this day to the birds of the air and to the wild beasts of the earth" (1 Samuel 17:46). This was young David's response to Goliath who first threatened him saying, "Come to me and I will give your flesh to the birds of the air and the beasts of the field" (1 Samuel 17:44). Similarly, Jeremiah the prophet spoke about the horrors of unburied bodies. "I will give their dead bodies for food to the birds of the air and to the beasts of the earth" (Jeremiah 19:7).

The honor and respect the Hebrews assigned to the human body, even when dead, motivated Mary Magdalene, Mary the mother of James, and Salome to go and anoint Jesus in his tomb (Mark 16:1). Their objective, however, was not realized because Jesus had already risen from the dead by the time they arrived at the tomb.

It is interesting to note that before Jesus' crucifixion, he approved of the custom of anointing the dead, for when an unnamed woman once anointed him with oil, he complimented her. "She has done what she could; she has anointed my body beforehand for burial" (Mark 14:8). Christians anointing the dead (a Judaic-religious custom) continued in the church well beyond the first century. By anointing the dead, the early Christians revealed they did not consider the deceased body as unclean, and neither did they believe, as the Romans did, that "the dead body was an abomination, abhorred by the gods."[8] Hence, Christians touched their dead relatives or friends without having to undergo ritual purification, as shown by the mid-third-century Syrian document *Didascalia Apostolorum* IV, 22:4.

The belief in the sanctity or dignity of the human body was also evident by Christians washing their dead. The book of Acts (9:37), for example, notes the friends of Tabitha (Dorcas) washed her expired body. And we learn from a New Testament apocryphal book (written about AD 200) that Marcellus took down the body of Peter (one of Jesus' twelve disciples) from the cross and then washed him with wine and milk (*Acts of Peter, The Vercelli Acts* 3:40).

Christians washing the dead continued for some time in the history of the church, for in the latter part of the fourth century St. Chrysostom (d. 407) noted that his fellow Christians even washed those who died of plagues (*Homily on St. John* 84). Moreover, the care and concern the early Christians extended to their dead was not just meant for their own. They also buried strangers. This impartial care that Christians extended to all deceased individuals greatly impressed the pagan Roman emperor, Julian the Apostate, despite his hatred for Christians, whom he derisively called "Galilleans." During his brief reign (AD 361–363), he wrote to Arsacium, his pagan high priest, saying the care Christians gave to all dead persons—Christians and non-Christians alike—was one of the reasons for Christianity's widespread growth. Honoring the dead and caring for their graves greatly impressed him (*Epistles of Julian* 49).

Julian's comments may seem odd to us in the twenty-first century. But they seem less odd when we remember that many Roman undesirables (called *infamia*), such as prostitutes, gladiators, undertakers, executed Roman criminals, slaves, and crucified victims, were usually not buried at all but discarded in ditches or left on roadsides, where they experienced "excarnation via animals and decay."[9] Regarding crucified bodies, the Romans usually did not even take them down from their crosses, let alone bury them.[10] Treating any of the dead in that manner was unthinkable to Christians. Thus, we find St. Augustine (early fifth century) urging his fellow believers to do all within their power to bury all the dead (*Sermo* 172:3). Even before Augustine's time, the high regard Christians had for the expired human body was not confined to their own bodies. One historian says of the Christians, "During the ravages of war, famine, and pestilence they considered it as their duty to bury the heathen as well as their fellow Christians."[11]

Why did St. Augustine and other early Christians devote so much care to the dead? One historian answered saying, "There was of course ... a theological reason for the Christian care of the dead, that is, the firm belief in a bodily resurrection ..."[12] Although Augustine said burial was indeed to be practiced, he did not say the dead person's resurrection depended on it. Rather, burial was a testimony of a Christian's faith in the resurrection. Hence, he wrote, "And if they [the pagans] do this [bury their dead] who have no faith in the resurrection of the body, how much more ought we, who have faith that a duty of this kind is due to a dead body that shall rise again and live forever?"[13]

In light of Christians believing in the sanctity of the human body—alive or dead—meant they did not see it as their own, free to do with it whatever they wished. This was another reason why cremating their dead was unthinkable. One historian remarked, "The main reason for [Christians] burying the dead was their respect for the body that was one day to rise to glory from the tomb."[14]

Almost a hundred years before Augustine, St. Antony (251–356) made known his high regard for a deceased human body when he addressed fellow Christians in Egypt, telling them that every dead person must be buried. His comments were in response to the custom some Egyptians had of keeping their embalmed/mummified dead relatives on couches in their homes, rather than burying them. To Antony's dismay, some Egyptian Christians were also mummifying their dead. And to get them to stop this pagan practice, he cited the burial precedent of Jesus, as well as the burials of the Old Testament patriarchs and prophets. He wanted them to do likewise. Not to do so, he argued, was "transgressing the law and Christian practice" (Athanasius, *Life of Antony*, 90).

The common refrain of many in today's secular society says, "It's my body and I have the right do with it as I wish." This is said by many women who support abortion on demand, by individuals who tattoo their bodies, and by many who choose cremation. It is a statement that reflects a mind-set totally at odds with the biblical view of the human being, for as we have just seen above, St. Paul told the Corinthian Christians, "You are not your own, for you were bought with a price" (1 Corinthians 6:19–20). Today, these words are either unknown or simply ignored, even by some Christians.

In spite of these words by Paul, some cremationists today argue that those who oppose cremation, especially Christians, given their belief in the dignity of the human body, honor the human corpse too much, almost revering it. One critic has likened the honor given to the deceased human bodies as a "reversion to the pagan funerary rites of ancient Egypt."[15] In response, it is helpful to note that while some of the pagan Egyptians embalmed/mummified their dead (as we have just seen), some even placed mummified bodies on couches in their homes, there is no evidence the high regard Christians had for the deceased body had anything to do with revering them. Moreover, it should not be forgotten the Hebrews (mentioned in the chapter 3) also greatly respected their dead, but they did not revere them. There is a significant difference between seeing the body as a sacred creation of God and revering it. The latter implies an attitude of worship; the former does not. Neither the Christians nor their Judaic ancestors revered their deceased relatives or friends. They would have seen such behavior as a gross violation of the first commandment that condemns worshiping or religiously revering anyone but God alone.

The city of Rome, according to the tenth table of the Twelve Tables of Roman law, had outlawed burials or cremations inside its walls, the *pomerium*. However, there were some exceptions because vestal virgins and prestigious dignitaries were usually buried or cremated within the city's walls. This legal ban, however, began to lose some of its force in the fourth century after Christianity had attained legal status in AD 313 and had grown in size and influence. Given that Christians saw the dead as part of the living, by the latter part of the fourth century, they began burying their dead in church yards. This meant they brought the dead close to the city's boundaries, near where churches were located. And soon "Roman towns [became] a network of Christian sacred sites."[16]

Finally, the high value Christians assigned to the human body in part also stemmed from their knowing that God himself valued the human body, for he had his only begotten Son come to earth in human flesh. As the apostle John wrote, "And the Word became flesh and dwelt among us" (John 1:14).

They Saw Death as "Sleep"

In addition to the early Christians having had a number of burial precedents from the Old and New Testament eras and their high regard for the human body, they also believed in the biblical doctrine that the dead were "asleep" in their graves. It was a doctrine that harked back to the prophet Daniel in the Old Testament. He declared that all the dead "who *sleep* in the dust of the earth shall awake" (Daniel 12:2, emphasis added). Jesus also taught death as sleep. He told one synagogue ruler, whose daughter had just died, "The child is not dead but asleep" (Mark 5:39). And on another occasion, he stated something similar to Mary and Martha when they came to him saying their brother Lazarus had died. He responded, "Our friend Lazarus has fallen asleep, but I go to awaken him" (John 11:11).

The Christian doctrine of death as sleep was also accented in the New Testament by St. Paul who, similar to Jesus, spoke of the dead being asleep and that Christ, who had been raised from the dead, was "the first-fruits of those who have fallen *asleep*" (1 Corinthians 15:20, emphasis added). And to the Christians in Thessalonica, Paul wrote, "For since we believe that Jesus died and rose again, even so, through Jesus, God will bring with him those who have fallen *asleep*" (1 Thessalonians 4:14, emphasis added).

The doctrine of death as sleep had a powerful effect among the early Christians. It was not an empty metaphor. They knew and believed the testimony of those who had seen Jesus after he had risen bodily from the dead. They also believed that at Christ's second coming they too would come forth from the grave, similar to Jesus' resurrection. Given this conviction, they took the Greek word *koimeterion* (meaning a temporary sleeping place) to replace the Greek word *necropolis* for a graveyard, and for the Latin-speaking Romans they transliterated *koimeterion* as *coemeterium*. It replaced the Latin word *area* for a graveyard. This verbal innovation had the function of comforting Christians regarding their future resurrection, and it also told the pagan Romans that God would someday resurrect not only Christians but all who were "asleep" in their graves, including them.

Interestingly, as shown in the next chapter, by mid-third century the pagan Romans began to use the word *koimeteria* or *coemeteria* (both plural) when they criticized Christian burial places. By using these words, the pagans ironically echoed the biblical doctrine of death as sleep and thus underscored the Christian conviction that someday there would a resurrection of the dead.

In addition to death seen as sleep in the Bible, it was also declared and confessed in the writings of Christianity's early church fathers. The Latin church father Tertullian mentions this biblical concept in his *De Anima*, written in about AD 197. So do the writings of St. Chrysostom (late fourth and early fifth century) and some of St. Augustine's writings (early fifth century). And early church documents also taught and proclaimed it, for instance, the *Didaskalia Apostolorum* (mid-third century Syrian liturgical document) and the *Apostolic Constitutions* (ca. AD 375).

The conviction that death is sleep is also revealed by inscriptions on countless gravestones and stone tablets found in many Christian catacombs in Rome, Naples, Syracuse, Malta, and several other sites. Some inscriptions read: *Hic Quiescet Severus* (here Servus rests); *Leo Hic Quiescet in Pace* (here Leo rests in peace); *Hyperechius Hic Dormit* (Hyperechius sleeps here); *Hic Requiescit in Pacis Flora* (here Flora rests in peace); *In Christo* (in Christ); *Pax Tecum* (peace be with you); and

In Pace (in peace).[17] Whether the inscription *In Pace*, found in many cemeteries, was once a part of a longer inscription, or only by itself, is not known. In either case, "It became an important identifying mark of a Christian burial."[18]

By way of contrast, Rome's pagan inscriptions revealed no hope beyond the grave.[19] The following epitaph was rather common among pagans in Rome: *Sit Tibi Terra Levis* (May the Earth Lie on You Lightly). This was often abbreviated as STTL.[20]

The Christian conviction that all dead persons are "asleep," awaiting their resurrection, was not confined to the early Christians. Even today (twenty-first century) one can still see inscriptions on gravestones in many church cemeteries, for instance, in North America, that read, "Asleep in Jesus," "Rest in Peace," "Sleep Softly," etc.

They Wanted to Return the Body to the Earth

When Adam and Eve fell into sin, God told both, "For you are dust, and to dust you shall return" (Genesis 3:19). These words were not forgotten by Christians in their opposition to cremation. Thus, by insisting on burying their dead, they wanted to return their deceased bodies from whence they came, to the bosom of the earth.[21] Similarly, Irenaeus (d. ca. AD 202), bishop of Lyons in Gaul (modern France), wrote, "Although it [the dead body] is dissolved at the appointed time, because of our primeval disobedience, it is placed, as it were in the crucible of the earth" (*Fragments from the Lost Writings of Irenaeus* XII).

In the fourth century, the church father Lactantius (240–320), known as "the Christian Cicero" who once tutored Crispus, son of Constantine the Great, criticized the Roman practice of casting executed criminals and other socially undesirable deceased individuals onto roadsides or into ditches instead of burying them. He declared, "We cannot bear that the image and workmanship of God should be exposed as a prey to wild beasts and birds, but we restore it to the earth from which it was taken" (*The Divine Institutes*, 6:12).

Early Church Fathers Opposed Cremation

When the early church fathers spoke against the practice of cremation, they did so in defense of inhumation. Their criticisms were never directed at fellow Christians, for none ever opted for cremation. This is a remarkable fact, because there were other pagan practices that the church fathers had to warn and admonish Christians not to imitate. But cremating their dead was not one of them.

As we have seen in chapter 4, apparently the first Christian who is recorded as having spoken against cremation was Minucius Felix, a Christian lawyer in Rome. In his dialogue *Octavius*, written in about AD 195, he has Octavius, a Christian with the same name as the dialogue's title, saying, "We adopt the ancient and better custom of burying in the earth. See, therefore, how for our consolation all nature suggests a future resurrection" (*Octavius* 34:11). These words were largely in response to the pagan critic Caecilius who earlier had angrily argued with Octavius. "They [Christians] execrate our funeral pyres and condemn cremation" (*Octavius* 11:4). These words document that Christians did more than just reject cremation; they even execrated and condemned it.

Another church father who addressed the practice of cremation was Tertullian (d. ca. AD 225), from Carthage in northern Africa. He not only opposed it but also attacked it because of its cruelty and violence. "I, on my side, must deride it [cremation] still more, especially when it burns up its dead with harshest inhumanity ... What pity is that which mocks *its victims* [sic] with cruelty?" (*On the Resurrection of the Flesh* 1). He also criticized cremation in another of his writings, where he argued the human body is "undeserving of an end which is inflicted upon murderers" (*A Treatise on the Soul*

51). Philip Schaaf, the nineteenth-century church historian, says Tertullian saw cremation as "a symbol of the fire of hell."[22]

Church Councils and Synods

Although many early church councils and synods commonly issued canons, for instance, against abortion in order to deter weak women from terminating pregnancies, they issued none for cremation. Why not? There was no need to do so because disposing of the dead by cremation was one cultural practice Christians did not try to imitate, not even in their weakest moments. There is not a single recorded instance of Christians having ever cremated their dead. One church historian said it well. "There was no legalized prohibition against cremation in Christian Antiquity. None was needed, for the Christians by reason of their belief abhorred it."[23] Similarly, Nikolaus Müller, another church historian, stated that no formal ban regarding cremation was necessary, because there was "an unwritten law" (*ungeschriebenen Gesetz*) that told Christians they were not to incinerate their dead.[24] They saw cremation as biblically and theologically wrong and sinful.

Christians spurned and abhorred cremation because it clashed with their biblically anchored beliefs, and for more than one reason. They, as already noted, had a high view of the human body. Cremation, given its violent and destructive nature, contradicted this conviction, for it treated the body similar to refuse. Moreover, cremation also departed from what had been done with Christ's dead body when he was laid in a tomb after his crucifixion.

Even though there are no records of any Christian in the early church having ever said that God could not resurrect a cremated body, Christians did not want to give any credence to the pagan Romans who falsely believed a cremated body could not be resurrected. That this pagan belief existed among the Romans is evident from one of the severe persecutions Christians experienced in AD 177 in Lyons, Gaul. Throngs of Christian-hating persecutors rushed into Christian homes, dragging their occupants into the marketplace "with every kind of maltreatment" and with "every torment that blood-thirsty imagination could devise."[25] Recalling this horrific incident, Eusebius (d. AD 339) reports after many of the Christians were killed and then burned at Lyons, their scorched bones, along with ashes, were cast into the nearby Rhone River, an act deliberately done by the pagans to mock Christianity's doctrine of the resurrection of the body. Eusebius quotes the persecuting mockers saying, "Now let's see if they'll rise again and if their god can help them and save them from our hands" (*Ecclesiastical History* 5:63).

Conclusion

It is clear when the early Christians went to Rome, they did not do as the Romans did. They consciously and deliberately went against the pagan culture in a number of ways. They evidently remembered St. Paul's words about not conforming to this world. Their consistent rejection of cremation is evidence that they saw it as contrary to the will of God. In addition, as Hans Lietzmann has noted, they reasoned,

> Might it [cremation] not give the world the appearance of denying the Christian faith in the resurrection? Was not this mode forced upon the martyrs by their pagan persecutors? The will of God, they believed, pointed to burial, for that was how Jesus was buried, and it was more loving and reverent. The body once housed the temple of the Holy Spirit, and therefore it must be reverenced accordingly.[26]

Thus, they remained stalwart in opposing and rejecting cremation. They stood apart. They did not conform to a pagan custom.

---

[1] I am indebted to Alan Kreider's comments and observations with regard to the significance of Christians as *paroikoi* vis-à-vis the pagan Romans. See his book *Worship and Evangelism in Pre-Christendom* (Cambridge, UK: Grove Books Limited, 1995). Although Kreider does not relate the concept of *paroikoi* to cremation, one can argue that this concept does shed additional light on understanding why the Christians opposed and rejected the pagan practice of cremation.

[2] Will Durant, *Caesar and Christ: A History of Roman Civilization from Their Beginnings to A.D. 325* (New York: MJF Books, 1944), 598.

[3] Alfred C. Rush, *Death and Burial in Christian Antiquity* (Washington, DC: The Catholic University of America Press, 1943), 247.

[4] Henri Daniel-Rops, *The Church of the Apostles and Martyrs* (London: J.M. Dent and Sons, 1960), 206.

[5] Norman L. Geisler and Douglas E. Potter, "Ashes to Ashes: Is Burial the Only Christian Option?" *Christian Research Journal* (July–September, 1998), 31.

[6] H. Richard Rutherford, "Honoring the Dead: Catholics and Cremation," *Worship* (November, 1990), 483.

[7] A. W. Argyle, "The Historical Christian Attitude to Cremation," *The Hibbert Journal* (October, 1958), 69.

[8] Paul Binski, *Medieval Death: Ritual and Representation* (London: British Museum Press, 1996), 10.

[9] Valerie M. Hope, *Death in Ancient Rome* (New York: Routledge, 2007), 162.

[10] Donald G. Kyle, *Spectacles of Death in Ancient Rome* (New York: Rutledge, 1998), 169.

[11] Philip Schaaf, *History of the Christian Church* (New York: Scribners and Sons, 1898), 2:381–82.

[12] James Stevenson, *The Catacombs: Life and Death in Early Christianity* (Nashville, TN: Thomas Nelson Publishers, 1978), 9.

[13] St. Augustine, "The Care To Be Taken For The Dead," in Roy J. Defarrari (ed.), *Saint Augustine: Treatises on Marriage and Other Subjects* (New York: Fathers of the Church, 1955), 383.

[14] Rush, op. cit., 247.

[15] William E. Phipps, "The Consuming Fire for Corpses," *Christian Century* (March 4, 1981), 222.

[16] R.A. Markus, *The End of Ancient Christian Antiquity* (New York: Cambridge University Press, 1990), 151.

17 Cited in Rush, op. cit., 21, 22.

18 Graydon F. Synder, *Inculturation of the Jesus Tradition: The Impact of Jesus on Jewish and Roman Culture* (Harrisburg, PA: Trinity Press, 1999), 118.

19 W. H. Withrow, *The Catacombs of Rome and Their Testimony Relative to Primitive Christianity* (London: Hodder & Stoughton, 1895), 59.

20 Ibid., 61.

21 Rush, op. cit., 247.

22 Schaaf, op. cit., 383.

23 Rush, op. cit., 247.

24 Nikolaus Müller, "*Koimeterein,*" *Realencyclopädie für Protestantische Theologie und Kirche* (Leipzig: J.C. Hinrichs'sche Buchhandlung, 1901), 10:815.

25 Hans Lietzmann, "The Christian Church in the West," *Cambridge Ancient History* (Cambridge: Cambridge University Press, 1939), 12:519.

26 Ibid.

CHAPTER 7

CREMATION'S RETURN TO THE WEST PRESENTS PROBLEMS FOR CHRISTIANS

Those who cannot remember the past are condemned to repeat it.
—George Santayana

When the early Christians in the first century arrived in Rome and its surrounding areas, they immediately encountered a major problem—namely, the longstanding practice of cremating deceased human beings. Given their Judaic background, along with their biblical knowledge and Christian convictions, they firmly opposed and rejected this pagan funerary custom. Their rejection soon became one reason the Romans despised and persecuted them. Despite the coercive power of culture, of which cremation was an integral part of the Roman Empire, the Christians did not acquiesce or succumb to it. Then soon after Christianity had received legal recognition in AD 313, Rome in the same century stopped cremating its human corpses. And with this secession, the problem of cremation for Christians in Rome had come to an end. Now they could bury their dead in peace and quiet, without ridicule or harassment from pagan neighbors. The Christian practice of inhumation soon became the cultural norm in the West after Christianity had spread to the northern regions of Europe.

Christianity's Anticremation Stance Again under Attack

The cultural serenity Christians enjoyed in much of the Western world by no longer being harassed or criticized for not cremating their dead from the fourth to the eighteenth century experienced its first-recorded interruption when a Mrs. John Pratt in 1710 in Ireland, as noted earlier, had herself cremated. Then, a hundred years later (mid-1800s), more cremations occurred in different parts of Europe, and by the late 1800s the cremationists had succeeded in permanently establishing cremation in Europe and in the United States.

Cremation once again presented problems for Christians as earth burial was verbally attacked by cremationists. Moreover, cremationists were not concerned about the likelihood that bringing back cremation would again result in falsely accusing Christians, as the pagans did in the Roman era, of believing that cremating a human body prevented its future resurrection. Despite, as already noted, Christians did not believe or teach that a cremated body could not be resurrected. Minucius Felix in his dialogue *Octavius* (ca. AD 195) had made that quite clear to Caecilius, Roman pagan, who had falsely accused Christians of that faulty belief. Minucius had Octavius tell him, "Nor, as you believe, do we fear any loss from burning, but we adopt the ancient and better custom of burying in the earth" (34:10). Nevertheless, for the pagans this specious argument was a convenient way to harass Christians.

Cremation Undermines the Doctrine of the Resurrection

Moreover, when the cremation movement became active in the mid-1800s, its promoters also showed no concern that cremation would likely undermine Christianity's doctrine of the body's future resurrection. And that did indeed happen. As Stephen Prothero, a pro-cremationist author, has recently stated, "Cremationists undermined the doctrine of the resurrection of the dead ... not so much by refuting it as by threatening to render it obsolete."[1] He further states that in the minds of many today, "It is the soul that is immortal, their [cremation] rite seemed to say, not the body."[2] Although Prothero does not specifically say whether the body's destruction in cremation prompts people to believe that only the soul is immortal, his discussion implies it.

In 1990, J. Douglas Davies in Britain found and reported, "The majority of those who believe in life after death do not believe in the resurrection of the body."[3] In light of this finding, Davies, although a cremationist, thinks, "Cremation services could be fostering disbelief in the doctrine of the resurrection because of the implied assumption that resurrection has to do with graves and cremation has practically nothing to do with graves."[4] And he further states that in traditional burial services the focus is on the body and its future resurrection, whereas in cremation services there is an implied message that the body is destroyed and gone forever, leading even many Christians to conclude that only the soul is immortal.[5] This explanation by Davies sheds considerable light on how cremation undermines Christianity's biblical and cardinal doctrine of the body's future resurrection.

In 2006, Scripps Howard News Service reported that 54 percent of Americans did not believe in a future resurrection of the dead, and 10 percent were undecided.[6] Since about 70 percent of the US population is classified as Christian, the figure of 54 percent that do not believe in the resurrection of dead clearly includes a sizable number of Christians who deny the resurrection. Here too it seems reasonable to ask whether the rising rates of cremation in the United States, especially in recent years, have influenced Americans, including many Christians, to no longer believe in the future resurrection of the body.

As Davies states, "Cremation triggers new thoughts about the future of the human self. The body is finished. This is the message of cremation. The ashes of cremation symbolize the fact of bodily dissolution rather than of the perpetuation of the deceased until some future day. In other words the ashes of cremation carry the opposite message from the remains of burial."[7] Hence, it is no surprise that denying the resurrection is to many, including some Christians, a consequence of cremation.

If cremation leads some Christians to no longer believe in the resurrection of the body but only in the survival of the soul, then these individuals have departed from historical, biblical Christianity. For to be a Christian is to believe in the physical resurrection of the body of which Christ's bodily resurrection was the "first-fruits," as St. Paul told the Corinthians. It was Christ's resurrection from the dead that brought Christianity into existence through the faithful efforts of his apostles who had personally seen the resurrected body of their Lord a number of times (about twelve) over a period of forty days, from Easter to Pentecost. The post-resurrection appearances of Christ transformed his disciples from weak followers to fearless proclaimers of what they had seen and heard. For instance, when Peter and John, after being released from prison, were told to stop preaching the Christian message that included the resurrection of Christ, they responded, "For we cannot help speaking about what *we have seen and heard*" (Acts 4:20, emphasis added). Physical threats or imprisonment did not muzzle their teaching or preaching, for history and tradition tell us that of the twelve apostles all but the apostle John (who died in prison) were executed for proclaiming that message. So convinced were they Christ had arisen from the dead that they vouched for it by signing their testimony in blood, so to speak. But if only the soul survives, as one observer asks, then why did God assume human flesh in his Son, Jesus Christ? Clearly, there would have been no need for Christ to suffer, die, and arise from the dead.[8]

Moreover, the doctrine of the resurrection of the body, based on Christ's own resurrection, is the linchpin of Christianity. But if cremation fosters a belief in only the survival of the soul, then that belief shatters Christianity's cardinal doctrine.

Cremation Contradicts Death as "Sleep"

It is impossible to envision a deceased person being asleep when he or she has been reduced to ashes and more so when the ashes have not even been buried but scattered on a body of water, in some flower garden, or on a golf course, shot into space, or mixed with the powder in fireworks. The Christian conviction of death as sleep is not an outdated or geographically isolated conviction. An article in 1999, "Deathly Concern: African Christians and Cremation in Zimbabwe," that discusses the disposal of the dead among Christians in Zimbabwe shows Christians there continue to see death as sleep, as they have from the time of Jesus and St. Paul. This article also notes that Zimbabwe Christians see cremation contradicting the belief of death as sleep. And the article further states that they "cringe at the thought of cremation."[9]

Cemetery as God's Acre

From their beginning, Christians always spoke of their buried fellow believers in words that conveyed a high degree of comfort and solace. This solace first came from Christ, who said that Lazarus, already dead for four days, was merely "asleep." It was a comforting response. And consistent with the concept of death as sleep, English-speaking Christians (as noted previously) coined the word "cemetery" (derived from the Latin *coemeterium,* a sleeping place) to testify that the dead were "asleep" until Resurrection Day. In German-speaking areas, Christians often called the cemetery *"Gottes Acker"* (God's Acre or God's Seed Field).

For Christians the cemetery as God's acre was not just a burial site. The gravestones in many Christian cemeteries portrayed messages that revealed those interred had been followers of Jesus Christ. These stones commonly revealed biblical passages, biblical art, or biblical verses that indicated lying in the grave was not forever but that body and soul would someday be reunited on the day of resurrection. These inscriptions date back to about the middle of the second century when many early Christians were buried in the catacombs in various areas of the Roman Empire.

The term God's acre or God's seed field may have its origin from what St. Paul wrote in 1 Corinthians 15 (the resurrection chapter), where he gives the analogy of a planted seed that dies and then brings forth a new plant. Using this analogy, he said,

> But someone will ask, "How are the dead raised? With what kind of body do they come?" You foolish person! What you sow does not come to life unless it dies. And what you sow is not the body that is to be, but a bare kernel; perhaps of wheat or of some other grain. But God gives it a body as he has chosen, and to each kind of seed its own body (1 Corinthians 15:35–38).

Then Paul continued, "So it is with the resurrection of the dead. What is sown is perishable; what is raised is imperishable. It is sown in dishonor; it is raised in glory ... It is sown a natural body; it is raised a spiritual body" (1 Corinthians 15:42–44). Thus, it is plausible that Paul's description of the resurrection led Christians to conclude that a cemetery, in addition to being a "sleeping place," was also God's acre or God's seed field, where dead human bodies are planted "seeds" that will someday bring forth new, glorified bodies, similar to Christ's resurrected body.

The analogy of a planted seed and the resurrection of the body is contradicted by cremation. For in cremation the seed (the dead body) is destroyed by fire and no longer capable of bringing forth a new growth. Paul's analogy of the planted seed and the resurrection of the body supports only earth burial, not cremation. Hence, cremation in contrast to the concept of God's acre presents another theological problem for biblically minded Christians.

Cremation: An Act of Destructive Violence

One of the facts of cremation that many people, including some Christians who favor it, evidently do not think about is that cremation is the ultimate form of violence known to mankind. Advocates of cremation apparently do not realize that fire in the Bible is, for the most part, a symbol of evil, destruction, and sometimes a portrait of hell, as in "the hell [*gehenna*] of fire" in Matthew 5:22.

Cremation is indeed violently destructive in its disposing of dead, helpless human beings. One need only recall how the body reacts to the fire of violence in a crematory's furnace, as noted in chapter 3. Being aware of cremation's destructive nature prompts the question: How can a spouse, relative, or friend do this to a loved one? Yet, because so many people seem not to think about the violent nature of cremation, they fail to ask this question, and so they conform to what others have done by subjecting a relative or friend to the most severe form of destructive violence on earth.

The Psalmist in the Old Testament asked God, "protect me from men of violence" (Psalm 140:1 NKJV). Although he asked to be protected from violence while he was alive, it can be argued that his plea is also relevant regarding the violence done to deceased humans when they are cremated.

Nearly a hundred years ago, the violent, destructive nature of cremation appalled Carl Ludwig Schleich (d. 1922), a German surgeon who pioneered infiltration anesthesia. Said he, "To destroy human cells by burning them is totally contrary to nature. Thus, we must decide to outlaw cremation, for it is the greatest error in civilization."[10]

Giving Spiritual Offense

Even if cremation were a matter of indifference, or an *adiaphron*, as some theologians call it, there is still a serious problem with it. It gives spiritual offense to many Christians and also to many non-Christians. However, giving spiritual offense regarding certain behavior is often ignored by many Christians today, in spite of what St. Paul pointedly said about it. He told the Christians in Corinth if someone who was weak in his faith and offended by a fellow Christian, for example, eating meat that had been sacrificed to pagan idols, then he must not eat that meat. Applying this admonition to himself, Paul said, "Therefore, if food makes my brother stumble, I will never eat meat, lest I make my brother stumble" (1 Corinthians 8:13).

Some years ago, while visiting in the home of a former university professor and friend of mine, together with his wife (both irreligious), I mentioned that a well-known Lutheran clergyman and denominational executive had himself cremated. They were visibly shocked because to them cremation was something that Christians, who believe in the resurrection of the body, did not do. To both, cremation was a spiritual "stumbling block," similar to what Paul said in 1 Corinthians 8:13. Hearing that a Christian had opted for cremation did not draw them closer to Christianity.

Many Christians, especially where they are a minority in mostly pagan regions, are also often spiritually offended when they hear some Christians in the West have had themselves cremated. This was cogently illustrated by the response of a former Christian missionary from India. When asked whether any Christians in India cremated their dead, he replied, "Positively not! Cremation is heathen. The Christians of India bury their dead because burial is Christian."[11] A similar reaction to cremation was reported from Kenya, Africa, where the wife of an Anglican archbishop in July 2002 was cremated. Kenyan Christians upon hearing this report uttered "gasps of astonishment," and the report further stated, "Most Kenyan Christians believe that the body should be buried because of the biblical example and their faith in the resurrection."[12]

Given that St. Paul told the Corinthian Christians not to eat meat sacrificed to idols if it offended other Christians and caused them to stumble spiritually, clergy and theologians would do well to heed Paul's words by telling today's Christians, many of whom think cremation is an acceptable option for them, that cremation does indeed spiritually offend many Christians both at home and abroad. If Paul felt it was necessary for Christians to stop eating meat dedicated to idols, would he not have also said something similar in regard to many Christians who are spiritually offended when they hear another Christian opted for cremation?

Cremation Minimizes Grieving

According to research, individuals who choose to have a family member cremated express less grieving at funerals than those who have the body of the deceased present at a funeral for burial. British theologian J. Douglas Davies explains the reduced grieving this way: "Ashes do not evoke emotion in the same way as the dead body, or even a grave does; they represent what might be called a post–person state of the deceased."[13] He further notes, "The dead body carries the identity of the deceased in an immediate way. It is specifically his or her body, capable of evoking a personal response from the survivors. The ashes present a less personal, more distanced, identity of the deceased."[14] Since cremation funerals reduce grieving and related responses, Davies raises the question of whether cremation eliminates the important therapeutic value that traditional-burial ceremonies provide the survivors.[15]

The physical setting in which many funerals for cremated individuals take place also appears to minimize grieving. The following is an apt description:

> Too often one is asked to meet at the crematory, and what then ensues is dismal: an unaccompanied funeral car glides noiselessly under the *porte-cochere*, the casket is transferred to a stainless steel *'hors-d'oeuvre'* trolley and wheeled into the [funeral home's] chapel, which looks more like a waiting-room in a university or college hospital than a dignified setting for the disposal of the dead.[16]

A setting of this kind does not evoke a lot of grieving among the deceased person's survivors.

There is still another variable related to cremations contributing to less grieving. Philippe Aries, a French analyst of death and dying, has found cremated individuals, compared to those buried in graves, are soon forgotten by family members.[17] Even when urns are buried in cemeteries, they are rarely visited.[18] Aries also found survivors rarely erect monuments in memory of their cremated relatives.[19]

Also related to the reduction of grieving is the surprising fact, not widely known, that some survivors never even make the effort to pick up the urn from the mortuary that contains their cremated relative. One report shows that about 5.7 percent of the urns filled with ashes are unclaimed at mortuaries.[20] In September 2012, a newspaper report revealed fifty-six boxes of cremated remains were found in a foreclosed mortuary in Dayton, Ohio. No one had claimed or picked up the urns with ashes from the mortuary that had lost its license a few months earlier.[21]

Unclaimed urns, according to one observer, reveal the pervasiveness of a death-denial culture.[22] And interestingly, when one asks funeral directors whether they have unclaimed urns on their premises, most say they indeed have a number of them.

In days gone by, as noted earlier, cemetery visits served wholesome purposes related to grieving. They reminded the survivors not only of the ties they had to their loved ones but also of the brevity and unpredictability of their own lives, and that someday they too would have to leave this vale of tears. For Christians who visited cemeteries there was also the reminder that someday "all who are in the graves," as Christ said, "will hear His voice and come out ... to the resurrection of life" (John 5:28–29 NKJV). But when a cremated person's ashes have been scattered on golf courses or tossed on a body of water, there are no visits, and there is nothing to remind survivors of their departed family member(s). This recalls the old adage, "Out of sight, out of mind."

"Ashes to Ashes," Not a Biblical Phrase

Many Christian clergy have for decades used the words ashes to ashes at funeral's committal phrase, "Earth to earth, ashes to ashes, dust to dust." These words first appeared in the Christian funeral ritual of the Church of England in its *Book of Common Prayer* in 1549. In time, these words also became part of funeral rituals used by other church bodies, and thus they have been heard by countless Christians at grave-side interments for nearly five hundred years. The words dust to dust have a solid biblical base because God told Adam right after the fall, "Dust you are and to dust you will return" (Genesis 3:19). And the words dust to dust are also found in Ecclesiastes 3:20, where it says, "All go to the same place; all come from dust, and to dust all return." But the words ashes to ashes are not in the Bible. The Bible never speaks about dead humans turning to ashes.

Even though the words ashes to ashes in committal rituals of funerals have no biblical foundation, many uninformed Christians think they are biblically derived. Thus, many Christians erroneously believe that these words make cremation a God-pleasing act. This faulty conclusion oddly enough is not just of recent origin. More than a hundred years ago, Sir Henry Thompson (a strong advocate of cremation) in 1874 in England invoked these words to justify his advocating cremation.[23] Doing so, he violated the context of the words ashes to ashes in the *Book of Common Prayer*. For preceding the statement, "Earth to earth, ashes to ashes, dust to dust" is the following statement. "Forasmuch as it hath pleased Almighty God, in his wise providence, to take out of this world the soul of our deceased brother; we therefore commit his *body to the ground*: earth to earth, ashes to ashes, dust to dust, looking for the general Resurrection on the last day" (emphasis added).

Clearly, there is nothing in this ritual that even hints at burning the human body. Instead, its words talk about committing the body "to the ground." Nevertheless, context notwithstanding, William Phipps, a cremationist, in recent years commended the Church of England for having been a leader in promoting cremation. He says the words ashes to ashes in the *Book of Common Prayer* have helped many Christians accept cremation by their having heard clergy saying them at funeral services.[24] These words may indeed have done what Phipps says but only because people did not (and do not) know that the prayer book's use of them does not refer to cremation. Thus, it is important to reiterate that using the words ashes to ashes to support cremation is a clear violation of the context in which they appear in the Church of England's *Book of Common Prayer*.

Given that the phrase ashes to ashes has no biblical basis, how then did it get into the funeral ritual of the Church of England and later into the funeral ceremonies of many other Christian denominations? While it is difficult to answer this question with complete certainty, one thing, however, is certain. There is no evidence that the words ashes to ashes in the *Book of Common Prayer* had anything to do with cremation. That is clearly evident from the ritual's context just cited. And there is no record that anyone in Christian circles in the mid–1500s in England or on the Continent said or wrote anything in favor of cremation. Moreover, Christians at this time in history still strongly opposed cremation. Burning a human body was not even remotely imagined by them.

One hundred years after the *Book of Common Prayer* had appeared, Sir Thomas Browne in the 1650s in Norfolk, England, studied human remains of burial urns in Britain from the Roman era. With regard to cremated ashes, he writes the early Christians in Britain "abhorred" cremation, and that they willingly submitted themselves "unto the sentence of God, to return *not unto ashes* [emphasis added] but unto dust again."[25] This reference clearly indicates Christians in ancient Britain did not believe their buried bodies would turn to ashes. And it provides further evidence that the words ashes to ashes in the *Book of Common Prayer* were not written with reference to cremation.

If Christians had believed that the dead body would someday turn to ashes, Browne would most likely have mentioned it in his book. Hence, it appears that the words ashes to ashes became a part of the funeral liturgy in the *Book of Common Prayer* not because its formulators believed the body would turn to ashes, but because "ashes to ashes" and "earth to earth," together with "dust to dust," served as a rhythmic alliteration.

Going back to the question of how these words might have entered the *Book of Common Prayer*, it is possible that the words of Abraham or Job might have had something to do with their origination. In pleading with God not to destroy Sodom and Gomorrah, Abraham expressed his unworthiness, saying: "Who am I but dust and ashes" (Genesis 18:27). Similarly, the suffering Job said: "I am reduced to dust and ashes" (Job 30:19 NKJV). But here it must be recognized that neither Abraham nor Job implied, much less said, that when the body decays in a grave it turns to ashes. Dust and ashes were biblical symbols of penance of unworthiness, and that is what these two patriarchs intended to convey.

It will likely never be known with certainty what source, if any, influenced the formulators of the *Book of Common Prayer* to coin the phrase ashes to ashes. In addition to the possibility that the words of Abraham and Job might have influenced the prayer book's editors, it is also possible that the words ashes to ashes might have come from the words of the early church father Origen (d. AD 254), who once did say the dead body gets reduced to "dust and ashes" (*Principiis* 3:6). If the composers of the *Book of Common Prayer* were influenced by Origen, they violated the context of his remarks, for he said nothing about burning the dead to ashes. Moreover, the consistent rejection of cremation by the early Christians does not permit one to conclude that Origen would knowingly have said anything in support of cremation. If he would have envisioned someone in the future might use his words to support cremation, he would most likely have been appalled, given that all Christians, before, during, and after Origen's time in the third century strongly opposed cremation.

While it is difficult to determine what source, if any, influenced the words ashes to ashes to become a part of the *Book of Common Prayer* in 1549, is not difficult to see how in time they crept into the funeral liturgies of other churches outside the Church of England, on the Continent, and in America. Actions on the part of one organization or institution are often adopted by other groups. Although it took some time, by the late 1800s some Lutheran churches in Germany, for instance, had cribbed the exact wording of "earth to earth, ashes to ashes, dust to dust" by literally translating them into German as *"Erde zur Erde, Asche zur Asche, Staub zum Staub."* But not all Lutheran churches in Europe adopted the words of the *Book of Common Prayer*. Hence, at least one Lutheran funeral liturgy of 1854 in the province of Silesia did not translate "ashes to ashes" into German from the English. Its rubric only indicated that some soil be tossed onto the body once it had been lowered into the grave.[26] But thirty years later (1884) Wilhelm Loehe's Bavarian *Agende fuer christliche Gemeinde des lutherischen Bekenntnisse* (An Agenda for Christian Congregations of the Lutheran Confessions) translated the English words verbatim into German. Then by 1895, in the United States, a German translation of the exact English phrase appeared in the funeral ritual of the Lutheran Church-Missouri Synod,[27] and by 1919 it had become a part of the liturgy of the Lutheran churches of the Iowa Synod.[28] In the following years it became a part of most every funeral liturgy in all Lutheran churches in the United States, and soon the phrase ashes to ashes became a part of the funeral rituals of most other American denominations, too. Hence, one finds them in the rites of the Roman Catholic, Presbyterian, Methodist, Baptist, Pentecostal, and most other churches as well.

The formulators of this committal phrase, and the various denominations that borrowed it from the *Book of Common Prayer*, surely did not anticipate that ashes to ashes might someday be heard erroneously as giving approval to cremation. Evidently, the formulators and the borrowers of this committal phrase liked its alliteration and thus made it a part of their prayer book's funeral ritual. But as an old saying goes, words have meanings. Thus, every Christian pastor who does not intend to give the false impression that cremation is an acceptable Christian option, would be wise by merely saying, "Earth to earth and dust to dust" and omit the words ashes to ashes. Thus, people would not hear these words convey a meaning never intended. Better yet, pastors would do well if they replaced the entire three-part committal phrase with a stanza or two from an appropriate funeral hymn.

The following two stanzas from the hymn, "This Body in the Grave We Lay," by Michael Weisse (1480–1534) would be an appropriate substitute. They read as follows:

> This body in the grave we lay.
> There to await that solemn Day
> When God Himself shall bid it rise
> To mount triumphant to the skies.

And so to earth we now entrust
What came from dust and turns to dust,
And from dust shall rise that Day
In glorious triumph o'er decay.

Jettisoning Beautiful Christian Hymns

The primary responsibility of the Christian church is to teach and preach the Gospel of Jesus Christ that brings the message of forgiveness, life, and salvation to everyone who repents and believes in him. With this in mind, Christian musicians have penned numerous hymns conveying comfort and assurance to Christians who will someday be laid to rest in God's good soil, and from where they will in the future rise to life eternal. Many Christian hymns underscore this doctrine. The following are three examples.

Martin Schalling in his hymn "Lord, Thee I Love with All My Heart" (ca. 1567) wrote,

That I may die unfearing,
And in its narrow chamber keep
My body safe in peaceful sleep
Until Thy reappearing.

Johann Heermann, recalling the biblical concept of the dead "sleeping" in their graves, penned the following words in his hymn, "O God, Thou Faithful God" (1630):

And let my body have
A quiet resting-place
Within a Christian grave;
And let it sleep in peace.

And not to be overlooked is the well-known hymn "All Praise to Thee, My God, This Night" (1695) by the English hymnist Thomas Ken. In one stanza he implores,

> Teach me to live that I may dread
> The grave as little as my bed.

These and numerous other hymns that speak about Christians lying in their graves, awaiting Christ's call to resurrect them, make no sense when people are cremated and their ashes are scattered onto a body of water or on some other site. Even when the ashes are buried, it sounds hollow, even deceptive, to speak of them as "sleeping." The metaphor simply does not fit. It does not make sense to say a cremated person's ashes are asleep or resting. Thus, many comforting Christian hymns at cremation funerals now are jettisoned, or if used, they clash with the biblical concept of the dead being asleep in their graves. And as cremation continues to increase among Christians, these spiritually comforting hymns are becoming a theological anomaly.

"Cremation Cemeteries," an Oxymoron

Today's funeral industry, accustomed to the language of earth burial, still uses language reflecting that practice when cremations are reported in obituary columns. So we read about "cremation cemeteries." As noted in chapter 6, the English word *cemetery* is derived from the Latin word *coemeterium* that meant a temporary sleeping place. Hence, to use the term cemetery today for bodies that have been burned and reduced to ashes, even if the ashes are buried, contradicts its etymology and why Christians initially chose that word. Interestingly, Christians who opt for cremation do not speak of cremated ashes being asleep. They seem to know it would sound ridiculous. Briefly stated, the term *cremation cemeteries* is an oxymoron.

Do Not Put the Lord Your God to the Test

When Satan told Jesus to throw himself down from the pinnacle of the temple, assuring him that God would send his holy angels to protect him (Matthew 4:6), Jesus responded, "You shall not put the Lord your God to the test" (Matthew 4:7). To be sure, God would have protected him, but Jesus rejected Satan's temptation because he knew such an act was putting God to the test. To Jesus, it was not a question of what God *can* do but what he, as God's obedient Son, must *not* do.

The incident of Christ's temptation is a powerful parallel to the argument one sometimes hears from some well-meaning Christian advocates of cremation. They defend their acceptance of cremation by saying, "An all-powerful God can resurrect a cremated body." Indeed, God can resurrect any and all cremated bodies. But similarly, as in the case of Jesus' temptation, it is not what God can do but what people must not do. Therefore, as Christ responded to Satan his tempter, so too Christian defenders of the biblical practice of earth burial should kindly but firmly say to the cremation advocates, "Do not put the Lord your God to the test."

Given that many modern Christians have not heard their pastors preach or teach against cremation, the argument that cremation is tempting God undoubtedly comes as a surprise. For at least a generation they have only heard and seen their clergy and congregations accepting cremation. They even know of some pastors or priests who in recent years opted to have themselves cremated. In fact, it is becoming quite common in obituary columns to read that some deceased clergyman, from some well-known denomination, had his body disposed of by cremation.

Conclusion

The above arguments in opposition to cremation are biblically based and buttressed with biblically supportable references and compatible logic. One of the present chapter's principal arguments asserts that cremation undermines and casts doubt on the biblical doctrine of the resurrection of the body. This cannot be denied, and it is astonishing that many Christians, including many clergy and theologians, appear not to recognize this documented fact. J. Douglas Davies said it well when he stated the symbolism of cremation, like its burial counterpart, affects the belief in the resurrection of the body. For belief in the resurrection of the body assumes burial and graves, whereas cremation does not.[29]

Since cremation undermines and casts doubt on the biblical doctrine of the resurrection, and in some instances fosters actual disbelief in the resurrection of the body, it is a major problem for biblically minded Christians. It is a problem that pastors and theologians really can no longer afford to sidestep or ignore, as they have for the longest time. For when the doctrine of the resurrection topples, Christianity becomes null and void, an empty shell. As St. Paul declared, "For if the dead are not raised, not even Christ has been raised. And if Christ has not been raised, your faith is futile, and you are still in your sins" (1 Corinthians 15:16–17).

---

[1] Stephen Prothero, *Purified by Fire: A History of Cremation* (Berkeley, CA: University of California Press, 2001), 71.

[2] Ibid.

[3] J. Douglas Davies, *Cremation Today and Tomorrow* (Bramcote, England: Grove Books, 1990), 35.

[4] Ibid., 13.

[5] Ibid., 33.

[6] See Scripps Howard News Service, April 2, 2006.

[7] Davies, op. cit., 33.

[8] "Ashes to Ashes: Dying on the Cheap," www.bjmaxwell.com/tag/cremation (accessed September 26, 2012).

[9] Ezra Chitando, "Deathly Concern: African Christians and Cremation in Zimbabwe," *Pretoria: The Society* (April, 1999), 13.

[10] Carl Ludwig Schleich, *Vom Schaltwerk Der Gedanken: Neue Einsichten und Betrachtungen über die Seele* (Berlin: S. Fischer Verlag, 1924), 275. Schleich's citation is my translation.

[11] Cited by James W. Fraser, *Cremation: Is It Christian?* (Neptune, NJ: Loiszeau Brothers, 1965), 15.

[12] *Friday Church News Notes*, Port Huron, Michigan (August 2, 2002).

[13] Davies, op. cit., 14.

[14] Ibid.

[15] Ibid.

[16] Julian Litten, *The English Way of Death: The Common Funeral Since 1450* (London: Robert Hale, 1990), 3.

[17] Philippe Aries, *The Hour of Death,* trans. Helen Weaver (New York: Alfred A. Knopf, 1981), 577.

[18] Philippe Aries, *Western Attitudes Toward Death: From the Middle Ages to the Present*, trans. Patria M. Ranum (Baltimore, MD: The John Hopkins Press, 1974), 91.

[19] Aries, *The Hour of Death*, op. cit, 577.

[20] "Special Report," Cremation Association of North America (1996/1997), 4.

[21] See www.fox19.com/story/19577981/boxes-of-cremated-remains-in-found-in-ohio-house (accessed September 23, 2012).

[22] Michael Marchal, *Parish Funerals* (Chicago: Liturgy Training Publications, 1987), 70. Denying death is discussed in greater detail in chapter 10.

[23] Sir Henry Thompson, "The Treatment of the Body After Death," *The Contemporary Review* (January, 1874), 327.

[24] William E. Phipps, *Cremation Concerns* (Springfield, IL: Charles C. Thomas, 1989), 58.

[25] Sir Thomas Browne, *Hydrotaphia or Urne Buriall* (London: Henry Brome, 1658), 10.

[26] Oswald Fruehbuss, *Entwurf einer Agende fuer die evangelische lutherische Kirche in der Provinz Schlesien* (Breslau, Poland: Verlag von Carl Dulfer, 1854), 144.

[27] Friedrich Lochner, *Liturgische Formulare* (St. Louis, MO: Concordia Publishing House, 1895), 116.

[28] Wilhelm Loehe, *Agende fuer christliche Gemeinden des lutherischen Bekenntnisse* (Chicago: Wartburg Publishing House, 1919), 304.

[29] Davies, op. cit., 13, 33.

CHAPTER 8

CHRISTIANITY'S BURIAL SYMBOLISM

O death where is your victory? O death where is your sting?

—St. Paul

Christ told his followers, "You are not of the world" (John 15:19), and he also told them, "Let your light so shine before others, so that they may see your good works and glorify your Father in heaven" (Matthew 5:16). Taking his words to heart, the early Christians were bound to distinguish themselves from those who were "of the world," namely, their pagan neighbors in the Greco-Roman world. And distinguish themselves they did. They did so in a number of ways. One way was how they conveyed their faith with symbols regarding death, dying, and burial practices. These all reflected their faith in the future resurrection of the dead.

Death as "Sleep"

As noted in chapter 6, the early Christians remembered and believed what Jesus had told Martha, whose brother Lazarus had been dead for four days. "Our friend Lazarus has fallen asleep, but I go to awaken him" (John 11:11). And they also knew St. Paul had told the Christians in Thessalonica that their deceased ancestors had "fallen asleep" (1 Thessalonians 4:14). Seeing death as sleep was one way Christians distinguished themselves from their pagan neighbors. It was also an important reason why they rejected cremation, because it contradicted the concept of death as sleep. A body lying in a supine position in a grave resembles a body lying asleep on a bed. Moreover, seeing death as sleep also clashes with the end result of cremation, its ashes. Thus, it is not surprising that Christians who today cremate their loved ones do not engrave cremation urns with "Asleep in Jesus," or "Rest in Peace." They know that such an epigram would be oxymoronic. Moreover, when the ashes of a cremated body are scattered, as is increasingly done today, there is nothing that can be inscribed.

Regarding the Christian conviction that death is sleep, one historian noted this concept "was extremely difficult to instill it into the minds of the pagans."[1] And then he added, "One cannot but help be impressed with the way in which the joyful concept of death as sleep influenced the lives of the first Christians."[2] The concept indicated that someday all, including pagans, would rise from the dead. It comforted Christians but greatly perplexed the pagans.

Graveyards as *Koimeteria* (*Coemeteria*)

The early followers of Christ sought to make the concept of death as sleep publicly known. So they (as noted earlier) astutely chose the Greek word *koimeterion* for a graveyard and transliterated it to *coemeterium* in Latin. In the Greco-Roman culture both words simply meant a temporary sleeping place. Christians chose the word *koimeterion* to replace the Greek word *necropolis* and *coemeterium* in Latin to replace *area,* for neither *necropolis* nor *area* reflected their faith that the dead were asleep in their graves until Christ would return to resurrect them.

The actual year when Christians first used the word *koimeterion* or *coemeterium* is not known, but we do know that the African church father Tertullian already used *coemeterio* in his *De Anima* (XLI) treatise, written in about AD 197. And Hippolytus, the

Greek-speaking presbyter in Rome, in his *Apostolic Tradition* (ca. AD 215) tells Christians not to overcharge when burying a poor person in a *koimeterion* (Article 40). Then about five years later, Hippolytus again used the word *koimeterion* in his *Refutatio Omnium Haeresium* (IX.12.14) when he referred to a catacomb in Rome to which Zephrynus (bishop) had appointed Callistus as administrator.[3]

Before the early Christians (still low in numbers) had chosen the Greek word *koimeterion* and the Latin word *coemeterium,* they had buried their dead "in pagan communal *areae,* either in individual or family tombs or in tombs belonging to funerary associations."[4] Numerous Roman burials, including those of some Christians in the first and second centuries, took place along roadsides, outside a village or city. Just outside of Rome, for instance, roadsides were lined with tombs, monuments, and mausoleums. Some of these are still visible today. They were linear graveyards, and according to tradition, St. Paul (executed in ca. AD 68) was initially buried on the roadside of Via Ostiensis, about three miles from Rome.[5]

Christians Practiced Impartial Burials

As we saw earlier, Christians saw the human body, even when deceased, as God's creation. And when it came to honoring the dead, Christians were no respecter of persons. They buried the poor, the destitute, strangers, and the well-to-do, whereas, among the pagan Romans only some of the poor, if they were part of a funerary association, were buried or cremated. Others, as shown in chapter 2, such as artisans, paupers, beggars, criminals, prostitutes, gladiators, undertakers, and slaves were usually not buried at all. These individuals were indiscriminately tossed into open pits (*puticuli*), located on the Esquiline Hill in the city of Rome.

The average size of a pit (vault) was about fifteen by twelve feet square and about thirty feet deep.[6] In the 1870s, Rudolpho Lanciani (pioneer archaeologist) and his crew excavated some seventy-five *puticuli.* He found a trench one thousand feet long and thirty feet deep. It contained "many hundred *puticuli* or vaults."[7] These vaults contained not just discarded human bodies but also animal carcasses, along with the filth and scrapings from off the streets.[8] In the city of Rome alone hundreds upon hundreds of human bodies each year were discarded as garbage.[9] Before Caesar Augustus's reign (31 BC to AD 14) these pits were rarely covered, hence emitting a nauseating stench, plus exposing the public to disease-breeding pollution.[10]

Given that Christians believed in giving everyone, regardless of social or economic status, a decent burial appealed to many pagan Romans, especially the poor and culturally underprivileged.[11] It showed them they were not mere castaways but individuals created by God. Burying the poor and strangers had the effect of many Romans seeing this practice symbolizing Christian charity, compared to the pagans who, as just mentioned, tossed the poor, strangers, and social outcasts into communal pits or left them lie on roadsides.

Catacombs as *Coemeteria*

We have already seen in chapter 6 that Christians renamed graveyards, and in doing so they made public their conviction the dead in their graves were asleep, awaiting their resurrection. It was also about this time that Christians in Rome spoke of "the *coemeterium ad Catacumbas.*" Initially, this expression specifically meant "the cemetery at the 'Sunken Valley' by the present church of San Sebastian on the *Via Appia* just to the south of Rome."[12] Other burial sites were referred to in a similar manner, for instance, *coemeterium ad Ursum Pileatum* (cemetery at the Capped Bear), or *coemeterium ad Clivum Cucumeris* (cemetery at the Cucumber Hill).[13] The Latin phrase *ad catacumbas,* at the sunken valley is derived from the Greek *kata* (down) *kumbas* (hollows), thus down by the hollows. However, it was not until the sixteenth century that the name *catacomb* came to be used for other subterranean cemeteries.[14]

Chapter 6 indicated when Christians replaced the word *necropolis* with *koimeterion* in Greek and the Latin term *area* with *coemeterium,* both names conveyed a theological meaning, and for that reason the pagan Romans did not like these two names. This was notably evident during Emperor Valerian's persecution of the Christians in AD 257–259 when he had his deputy-prefect Aemilianus command Dionysius (a Christian bishop) that the Christians were not to assemble or enter *"ta kaloumena koimeteria"* (the so-called cemeteries).[15] Given that this Roman official said "the so-called cemeteries," he revealed that he disliked the Christian term *koimeteria* for graveyards. Even though he clearly disliked the term, he nevertheless used it. Evidently, by this time (mid-third century) the name *koimeteria* had become the cultural term for graveyards, indicating a major Christian influence.

As a pagan, this must have pained the deputy-prefect. Hence, it can be argued when Christians renamed the Greek word *necropolis* and the Latin word *area,* it was a stroke of genius.[16] For every time pagan Romans said *"koimeterion"* or *"coemeterium"* they spoke like Christians regarding the status of the dead, even though they did not believe what these two words meant.

In time, the word *coemeterium* among the pagan Romans lost its early Christian meaning when it merely became a name for a collective burial site. This loss is especially present today because most English speakers, including Christians, do not seem to know that the word *cemetery* in English is etymologically derived from *coemeterium* in Latin. They also do not realize every time they utter the word cemetery they are referring to something more than a collective burial site. Instead, they are proclaiming a theological message, namely, that all dead humans are "asleep" in their graves until Christ will resurrect them (John 5:28).

Catacomb Burials

In the latter half of the first century, the early Christians apparently buried their dead with the pagan Romans who did not cremate their dead, as is evident from the initial burial of the apostles Paul and Peter. Later, in the second century, Christians had their own *coemeteria*. Some of these were above ground. But given that Christians were despised people, they also wanted some of their cemeteries to be less conspicuous in order to avoid undue attention.[17] This led to their cutting graves in the soil of the upward slopes of sunken valleys (hollows), and then they interred their dead in these subterranean cemeteries (catacombs). These cemeteries became quite numerous, especially in the vicinity of Rome. Christians used these underground burial sites notably during the second, third, and early fourth centuries when many of them were often persecuted, and some were even martyred, as archaeological research has recently shown.[18]

The question is sometimes asked: How did the Christians turn these underground cemeteries into multiple tunnels or galleries, often on several levels? Constructing the galleries and digging out shelf-like spaces (*loculi*) for graves in their walls was done by workers known as *fossores*. Initially, these workmen were paid by church officials, but later, in the fourth century, many operated as independent entrepreneurs.[19]

Another question often asked is: How many Christians are buried in the catacombs, for example, in Rome? W. H. Withrow estimates that "about three million eight hundred and thirty-one thousand"[20] are interred there. He also states the entire Christian population in Rome was buried there over a period of at least three hundred years.[21] A more recent (1996) estimate lists an even higher number, namely, that the catacombs in Rome had galleries extending one thousand kilometers (600 miles) that provided burial space for about six million Christians.[22]

It is worth noting that of the multiple thousands of Christians buried in the catacombs, not a single urn with ashes has ever been found for a deceased Christian, except for some martyrs who were executed and burned against their will. Polycarp, who was burned at the stake in AD 156, is an example. This provides additional evidence that no Christian ever opted for cremation.

And it is interesting to know that initially many of the catacombs were privately owned by some prosperous Christians. This is evident in that the earliest catacombs bore the names of individuals, for instance, "Domitilla, Priscila, Praetextatus, Bassilla, and Trasone."[23] Then by the latter part of third century, the church began to own and administer some of them. The first example appears to have been the cemetery of St. Callistus in Rome when bishop Zephrynus in about AD 210 appointed Callistus to administer this cemetery.[24] He had been a former slave. Later, he served as bishop of Rome from 218-223.

The catacombs were exceedingly valuable to Christians for at least three centuries. But by the mid-fourth century relatively few Christians were laid to rest in them, a phenomenon made possible by the Edict of Milan (AD 313) that had granted Christianity legal status and freedom to practice its beliefs, including freedom to use above-ground cemeteries. And with Alaric's sacking of Rome in AD 410 the catacombs largely experienced neglect and disuse.[25] Then, for a thousand years they were forgotten until accidentally rediscovered in 1578 by unnamed individuals. Since their rediscovery, the mere mention of the word *catacombs* to many symbolizes early Christians burying their dead in cemeteries not visible to their pagan despisers. And Christians burying their dead in the catacombs also symbolizes their tenacity in rejecting Rome's culturally accepted practice of cremation.

Urbanization of the Dead

The early Christians insisted that "the dead were not polluting, and that their deaths and funerals were occasions for displays of hope, not resignation or fear."[26] And given that the early Christians were mostly urban residents, they commonly buried their dead by their churches, located near the city.[27] Thus, by the middle of the fourth century, "Rome was encircled by Christian cemeteries."[28] Peter Brown calls it the urbanization of the dead.[29]

Urban burial was "the most startling reversal of ancient practices."[30] Dealing with the dead in this manner was revolutionary, and it angered the pagans. It also angered Julian the Apostate emperor (ruled 361–363), for he saw himself "confronted with a religion [Christianity] which, in its foundation stories, has the dead and risen body as the central object of worship and veneration."[31] Adhering to the Greco-Roman belief that the dead were unclean, he sternly scathed Christians for how they honored the dead and where they buried them.

> You keep adding many corpses, newly dead, to the corpses of long ago. You have filled the world with tombs of sepulchers … The carrying of the corpses of the dead through a great assembly of people, in the midst of dense crowds, staining the eyes of all with ill-omened sights of the dead. What day so touched with death could be lucky? How, after being present at such ceremonies, could anyone approach the gods and their temples?[32]

But Julian's criticism did not deter the Christians, for by the end of the fourth century their dead had fully "colonized the central places [cities] of the living."[33] And even where Christians maintained their extramural cemeteries, they "proclaimed their separate and theologically different status."[34] Whether they interred their dead in or outside the city, they also provided "their own burial services as a corporal work of mercy without hired pallbearers or other assistants, even in times of plagues, when deaths were heavy and the funerary duties onerous."[35] Doing so, they again distinguished themselves from their pagan neighbors.

Funerals in Churches

One observer of early Christianity remarked, "Nothing more clearly distinguished the early Christians from their pagan neighbors than the reaction of the believers to the fact of death. They did not sorrow for the dead as others who had no hope. To die was to depart and be with Christ."[36] They apparently remembered St. Paul's words that told Christians in Thessalonica "not to grieve as others who have no hope" (1 Thessalonians 4:13). With that faith and disposition, they commonly brought their departed loved ones and friends into the church building before they buried them. As Alfred C. Rush has remarked, "from the very beginning the Christian funeral was a religious service ... with a joyful concept of death." Whereas, to pagans, according to Rush, "death was regarded as an evil."[37]

It has been said, "The Christian Church was born in song."[38] Two of the four gospels, Matthew and Mark, note that the night before Jesus' crucifixion, he and his disciples left the upper room to go to the garden of Gethsemane, and they sang a hymn. Although there is no formal Christian burial liturgy on record before AD 900, there are references from the early third century that indicate Christians sang Psalms at funeral services. St. Cyprian, bishop of Carthage (249–258), gives an account of Christians joyfully singing Psalms as they processed at night with torch lights carrying the bodies of martyrs to a cemetery.[39] Soon after writing this report, Cyprian too was martyred in 258 during Valerian's persecution (257–259).

Death as *Dies Natalis*

Another noteworthy conviction that set Christians apart from the pagan Romans was that death to them symbolized their *dies natalis* (day of birth). It was their birth into eternity with God. It was a day of joy. A prime example reflecting this belief was Ignatius, third bishop of Antioch, an Apostolic Father, martyred between AD 107 and 117 under the emperor Trajan (ruled 98–117). His persecutors tossed him to the lions in the Coliseum in Rome. While on his way to Rome from Antioch, and under guard, pending his execution, he wrote several letters to Christians in different locations, most of them in Asia Minor. He is often known as the first Christian who used the word *catholic* in regard to the church being the universal body of Christ. As the hour of his death drew near, he said "the pains of birth are upon me" (*Third Epistle to the Romans* VI). The belief in *dies natalis* is also found expressed a hundred years after Ignatius when Tertullian wrote, "We make offerings for the dead as birthday honors" (*De Corona* 3).

Epigraphic Symbols

Whether in catacombs or in above-ground cemeteries, evidence abounds with regard to Christians having left messages of their faith on the walls inside the catacombs or on grave stones on above-ground cemeteries. One noteworthy example is the Greek word ICTHUS, meaning fish. Christians used the word ICTHUS as a theological acronym, *Iesos Christos Theou Huios Soter*, translated as JESUS CHRIST GOD'S SON SAVIOR. Sometimes only the outline of a fish is etched on a stone tablet, and other times the word ICTHUS is followed by the word ZWNTWN (zoontoon), meaning "of the living," thus rendering it as JESUS CHRIST GOD'S SON SAVIOR OF THE LIVING, or simply FISH OF THE LIVING.[40]

There are also numerous other portrayals in the catacombs, such as painted frescoes depicting various individuals in the Bible and biblical accounts. For example, 108 portrayals of Jonah and the fish symbolizing the resurrection of Christ have been found in sixty catacombs of Rome.[41] These portrayals of Jonah again reveal that the early Christians, unlike their pagan neighbors, saw death as the precursor to their future resurrection. It was this faith that motivated them to draw, paint, and inscribe pictures of Jonah and the fish on catacomb walls.[42] Regarding the funerary art on sarcophagi and in catacombs, archaeologists have found that some of the art served as "a significant means of marking a Christian identity of resistance during the years of persecution in the third and fourth centuries."[43]

A Corpse's Feet-First Exit

Most people in the West know that a deceased person is commonly carried out feet first when taken from his or her home, church building, or to the cemetery. In English-speaking contexts the expression "they carried him out feet first" is an alternate way of saying he has died. This old expression, according to Sir Thomas Browne, a seventeenth-century Brit, reflects the Christian belief when a person dies, he or she is leaving the world with no desire to come back. Browne contrasts this custom with the Muslim practice of carrying the dead person out head first. The Muslim custom symbolizes looking forward to returning to earth to a delightful life again.[44] Carrying the deceased feet first is, of course, only a meaningful symbol when the person is buried rather than cremated. In the latter instance, the expression makes no sense.

East-West Axis of Christian Graves

Another burial symbol early Christians sought to convey was the direction their graves faced. The *Didascalia Apostolorum* (mid-third century Syrian document) specifies that the deceased person be placed in the grave in a supine position with his or her head at the west end facing east. This alignment of Christian graves has also been found elsewhere. Recent research at a major burial site of three to four thousand graves of an early Christian community at Kellis, Egypt, shows Christians in the mid-third century also aligned their graves on an east-west axis.[45] Whether this kind of alignment was already done by Christians in the first century is not known. But it is possible they did, especially if their reason for east-west graves stemmed from their belief when Christ comes to summon the dead from their graves, they will rise facing east. It has been conjectured that the following words from Matthew's gospel prompted this burial practice. "For as the lightning comes from the east and shines as far as the west. So will be the coming of the Son of Man" (Matthew 24:27). And often when Christians were not able to align their graves in an east-west position, but on a north-south axis, the deceased person was laid in the grave on his or her side facing eastward.

Although the early Christians in different geographical areas dug their graves on an east-west axis, there is no record indicating this practice was a firm requirement. Moreover, the catacomb walls did not always make it possible to follow this custom, for many of the walls did not run in a straight south-to-north direction permitting perpendicular graves dug east to west. Some catacomb walls curved. Many graves often pointed to the north, northwest, and northeast, or to the south, southwest, and southeast. Thus, east-west graves are largely a phenomenon of above-ground cemeteries.

The east-west axis of graves in time spread to other parts of the world where Christianity had a significant presence. For instance, when Christians had gained a foothold among the Vikings around AD 1000, they, along with forbidding cremation, "required simple earth or wooden graves oriented east-west."[46]

Whether cemeteries are located in Europe or in the Americas, the east-west graves still predominate, even though not all cemeteries reflect this custom. In today's highly secularized world, many Christians are no longer conscious of or do not give much thought to the east-west position of most graves. Some no longer know or recognize this Christian symbol. However, to the early Christians this burial symbol was significant and meaningful. It testified to their faith in the bodily resurrection. But with the rising rates of cremation that no longer require graves, this once-significant Christian symbol has become irrelevant. Even if an urn is buried in a cemetery, it cannot symbolize an east-west axis. Thus, cremation is contributing to the loss of another Christian symbol, centuries old.

Conclusion

Human beings are symbolically oriented creatures. They are the only creatures who are able to create symbols and assign them given meanings. It is part of their human nature, given to them by God when he created mankind. It is with symbols that human beings communicate with one another. And Christians, early in their history, devised symbols to communicate and underscore their unwavering faith and conviction that all, Christians and pagans, would someday arise from their graves, as Christ arose. To them the inevitable day of death was not awaited with fear or trepidation but with joyful anticipation. Their burial symbols sought to convey that faith and conviction both to themselves and to their companions in the faith who would follow them.

---

[1]   Alfred C. Rush, *Death and Burial in Christian Antiquity* (Washington, DC: The Catholic University Press, 1943), 15.

[2]   Ibid., 23.

[3]   There has been considerable debate whether Hippolytus is the rightful author of these two works, especially regarding *Apostolic Tradition*. But many scholars do now see him as the likely author of *Refutatio Omnium Haeresium*.

[4]   Nicolai, Vincenzo Fiocchi, Fabrizio Bisconti, and Danilo Mazzoleni, *The Christian Catacombs of Rome* (Regensburg, Germany: Verlag Schnell and Steiner, 1999), 13.

5   Robert W. Habenstein and William M. Lamers, *The History of American Funeral Directing* (Milwaukee, MN: Bulfin Printers, 1962), 70.

6   Keith Hopkins, *Death and Renewal: Sociological Studies in Roman History* (New York: Cambridge University Press, 1983), 2: 208.

7   Rudolpho Lanciani, *Ancient Rome in the Light of Recent Discoveries* (Boston, MA: Houghton Mifflin and Company, 1891), 64.

8   Ibid.

9   Bernard Green, *Christianity in Ancient Rome: The First Three Centuries* (New York; T & T Clark, 1971), 177.

10   Harold Whetstone Johnston, *The Private Life of the Romans* (Chicago: Scott Foresman and Company, 1905), 317.

11   Green, op. cit., 178.

12   J. M. C. Toynbee, *Death and Burial in the Roman World* (Ithaca, NY: Cornell University Press, 1971), 235. Toynbee translates *"Catacombas"* as "Sunken Valley."

13   Ludwig Hertling and Englebert Kirschbaum, *The Roman Catacombs and Their Martyrs*, trans. Joeph Costelloe (Milwaukee, MN: The Bruce Publishing Company, 1956), 17.

14   Green, op. cit., 182.

15   Eusebius, *Ecclesiastical History* (Cambridge, MA: Harvard University Press, 1942), 2:158.

16   Some scholars contend when Christians first used the word *koimeterion* or *coemeterium*, the name only referred to the burial place of individual martyrs rather than to graveyards as collective burial sites. This argument is questionable, for, as shown above, when Hippolytus in about AD 215 urged Christians to not overcharge for burying the poor, he used the term *koimeterium* as the place where they would be buried, and it does not appear he was talking only about the burial of martyrs. And, as also noted above, when Emperor Valerian's deputy-prefect referred to Christian burial grounds as "so-called cemeteries," he certainly had in mind more than the graves of martyrs.

17   Matilda Webb, *The Churches and Catacombs of Early Christian Rome: A Comprehensive Guide* (Portland, OR: Sussex Academic Press, 2001), xiv.

18   L.V. Rutgers, *Subterranean Rome: In Search of the Roots of Christianity in the Catacombs of the Eternal City* (Leuwen, Netherlands: Peeters, 2000), 9.

19   Ibid., 68.

20   Withrow, op. cit., 21.

21   Ibid., 22.

22   B. D. Shaw, "Seasons of Death: Aspects of Mortality in Imperial Rome," *Journal of Roman Studies* (1996), 101.

23   Green, op. cit., 181.

24 James Stevenson, *The Catacombs: Life and Death in Early Christianity* (New York: Thomas Nelson Publishers, 1978), 25.

25 Green, op. cit., 134.

26 Jon Davies, *Death, Burial and Rebirth in the Religions of Antiquity* (London: Routledge, 1999), 198.

27 Rutgers, op. cit., 10.

28 Green, op. cit., 185.

29 Peter Brown, *The Cult of the Saints: Its Rise and Function in Latin Christianity* (Chicago: University of Chicago Press, 1981). Brown says the urbanization of the dead was largely a phenomenon in the West. In the East the shrines of the martyrs were mostly located in extramural cemeteries.

30 Davies, op. cit., 195.

31 Ibid.

32 Cited in ibid.

33 Ibid., 194.

34 Ibid.

35 Habenstein and Lamers, op. cit., 62.

36 A. W. Argyle, "The Historical Christian Attitude to Cremation," *The Hibbert Journal* (October, 1958), 68.

37 Rush, op. cit., 170–174

38 Ralph Martin, *Worship in the Early Church* (Westwood, NJ: Fleming H. Revell, 1964), 39.

39 During the first four centuries, Christians conducted their funeral services at night in conformity with Roman customs and law.

40 Withrow, op. cit., 255.

41 Graydon F. Snyder, *Ante Pacem: Archaeological Evidence of Church Life Before Constantine* (Macon, GA: Mercer University Press, 2003), 7.

42 James D. Tabor and Simcha Jacobovici, *The Jesus Discovery: The New Archaeological Find that Reveals the Birth of Christianity* (New York: Simon and Schuster, 2012), 80.

43 Jas Elsner, *Imperial Rome and Christian Triumph: The Art of the Roman Empire AD 100–450* (New York: Oxford University Press, 1998), 139.

44 Sir Thomas Browne, *Hydrotaphia or Urne Buriall* (London: Henry Brome, 1658), 58.

45 Gillian Bowen, "Early Christian Burial Practices at Kellis, Dakhleh Oasis, Egypt," *The Artefact* (Vol. 26, 2003), 79.

46 Johannes Brondsted, *The Vikings,* trans. Kalle Skov (Harmondsworth, UK: Penguin Books, 1965), 290.

CHAPTER 9

THE GREAT CAPITULATION: CHURCHES ACCEPT CREMATION

Fortune favors the bold, but it abandons the timid.
—Latin Proverb

When despisers of earth burial brought cremation back to the West from the pagan Roman era in the last quarter of the 1800s, it made only minimal progress for a number of decades. Still strongly influenced by Christianity's longstanding opposition to cremation, most Westerners saw cremation as unthinkable. But as shown in chapter 1, that changed in the 1960s when cremation rates notably began to increase each ensuing decade.

Secular Culture Promotes Cremation

There is a saying, if fish could think, the last thing they would discover is water. Moving from fish to people, who can think but frequently do not, the last thing they seem to discover is culture. Fish are immersed in water. People are immersed in culture. Yet neither is conscious of how their environment (water for fish and culture for people) influences and affects their daily lives. Culture to most people is a hidden phenomenon. They are rarely conscious of it, and when they are, it is not for long. Thus, they accept and conform to their society's values, beliefs, and practices, and they are usually quite comfortable doing so.

For nearly two thousand years, cremation was a theological and cultural taboo among Christians. But in recent decades it has attained an acceptable cultural status that is now influencing increasing numbers of Christians to opt for it. It is also interesting that the culture of cremation has been quite successful in keeping people ignorant of Christianity's centuries-long rejection of cremation, an ignorance that further legitimates and enhances its increasing presence.

I define culture as a society's established beliefs, values, knowledge, and practices. Culture functions as a powerful social force that directs and shapes the behavior of individuals who are regularly in contact with it. Given the nature and power of culture, God through his Word has always cautioned his people to be aware of worldly or ungodly culture. In the Old Testament he told the Israelites not to adopt the pagan cultural practices of their neighbors, and in the New Testament God inspired St. Paul to write, "Do not be conformed to this world, but be transformed by the renewal of your mind, that by testing you may discern what is the will of God . . ." (Romans 12:2).

As noted earlier, the early Christians heeded these words when they rejected Rome's culturally approved practices of abortion, infanticide, and child abandonment. Rejecting cremation was another example of their not conforming to Rome's pagan culture. They acted similar to some Christians in the book of Acts who were accused of having "turned the world upside down" (Acts 17:6). Thus, by about the mid-fourth century, through Christian influences, apart from any church-council canons, cremation came to an end in Rome. Then, in the latter part of the eighth century cremation was formally outlawed in the Holy Roman Empire by Charlemagne the Great in the Paderborn Capitularies of Saxony in 785. This law decreed to end cremation among pagan enclaves in geographically isolated areas, particularly in the Saxon territories at the time.[1] The

Paderborn Capitularies also stated Saxon Christians were to be buried in church cemeteries and no longer in pagan burial grounds.[2]

Clergy and Churches Acquiesce

As church historians know, not long after Christ ascended to heaven doctrinal conflicts and divisions soon plagued the church. There were the Gnostics, Docetists, Arians, Donatists, Nestorians, and others who departed from the biblical teachings of Christ's apostles. Among these heretical groups, however, one does not find any of their followers accepting or advocating cremating their dead, not even the Gnostics, who saw the human body as consisting of evil matter, and they also denied the physical resurrection of the body. The Docetists, who taught that Christ did not have a material body but only appeared to have one, also did not engage in cremating their dead. And none of the other heretical groups who claimed to be Christians ever seemed to question the Christian opposition to cremation.

Given the decades of the Enlightenment's secular presence in Western culture, it has been quite successful in getting today's clergy and churches to acquiesce and conform to the pagan practice of cremating the dead. Reference has already been made with regard to the Roman Catholic Church and the Church of England, both of which formally accepted cremation in the 1960s. And since then nearly all Christian denominations have followed suit, with the exception of the Eastern Orthodox churches.

Acquiescing to cremation on the part of Christian clergy began in the early years of the cremation movement in the 1870s. When The Cremation Society was organized in England in 1874, a number of British clergymen joined its ranks the same year.[3] Nor was the early acquiescence of the clergy confined to the Church of England, for some Roman Catholic priests in Italy in the 1870s also offered little or no opposition to incineration. "In the capital of Lombardy a distinguished prelate even declared that the burning of the dead is in no wise contradictory to the dogma of the church."[4] In addition, many Italian priests accompanied bodies that were being taken to the *Tempio Crematorio,* where they offered prayers.[5] And as indicated earlier, Pope Paul VI acquiesced to cremation in 1963 when he in *de Cadaverum Crematione* (Concerning Cremation of the Dead) announced his approval of cremation. To justify his acquiescence he said the "souls will be reunited with their bodies" on the day of resurrection even if Christians are cremated.[6]

Had anything changed biblically in order for the pope to make this about-face from previous papal announcements that condemned cremation three times in the late 1800s and again in 1926? The answer is *no*! What changed was the Roman church's position, prompted by the secular culture, a powerful social force that preempted biblical theology and centuries of Christian rejection of cremation.

In 1997, the Roman Catholic Church went even further in its cultural capitulation when in Canada the Holy See granted permission to have the ashes brought into the church for a funeral service. A similar acquiescence has taken place in virtually all Protestant churches, even those in conservative denominations. For the most part, they all voice a similar response when they say the Bible does not prohibit cremation. Similar to the papacy and the Roman Catholic Church, they have conformed to the secular culture.

Sometimes one reads that the Eastern Orthodox churches, contrary to most other denominations, do not permit cremation. For the most part this is true. But upon closer examination, one finds some ambivalence in some of the Orthodox churches' literature. For instance, ethicist John Breck of the Greek Orthodox Church writes, "Neither the canonical nor the dogmatic tradition of the Orthodox Churches prohibits cremation."[7] However, he does say that within his church body some have been denied burial rites for choosing cremation, but even after saying this, he states that, "Laws in some countries and states (Japan, Louisiana) require cremation in certain regions, and such laws should be respected."[8] An article titled "Cremation" in *A Dictionary of Greek Orthodoxy* (1984) reveals a similar ambivalence when it states, "There is no definite dogmatical basis on which the stand of the Church against cremation can be unshakably supported."[9] But then the dictionary goes on to say, "In spite of the fact that there is no synodical binding decision of pan-Orthodox authority against cremation, there are definite opinions against it. And there are definite rulings prohibiting cremation, on the penalty of the departed Orthodox being deprived of the funeral and burial rites."[10] In its conclusion the article states that members of the Orthodox Church should seek their answer regarding cremation in the church's "life and tradition rather than in dogmatical arguments."[11]

On the other hand, the following account of the Orthodox church in Greece is noteworthy. In 1987, in Athens, Greece, about one thousand people died in an extreme heat spell. Given there were so many dead, the mayor asked the archbishop of the Church of Greece to rethink his opposition to cremation and permit this large number of deceased Greeks to be burned, because he felt the situation posed health hazards. The archbishop denied the mayor's request.[12] This archbishop's stand on cremation in Athens, however, differs from what the archbishop of the Syrian Orthodox Church in the United States has said regarding cremation. According to him, "The Syrian Orthodox Church does not have an official position on cremation. We do not encourage it. Our priests will conduct the funeral services at the church according to the rites of the Church but will not attend the cremation."[13]

In spite of these somewhat-differing positions in Orthodox churches, it should be noted that there are some individual priests and archbishops, unlike most clergy in other denominations, who do take a firm stand in opposition to cremation. For instance, the archbishop of the Russian Orthodox church has not hesitated to state, "Those who do not know God's will or are indifferent to it or are consciously opposed to it, burn their bodies."[14] He has also stated cremationists are guilty of "divine disobedience."[15] Similarly, the rector of the Russian Orthodox Cathedral of St. John the Baptist, Washington, DC, boldly declares, "At the root of the recent practice of cremation lies the denial of eternal life. The practice is anti-Christian. The faithful children of the Orthodox Church must flee from it."[16] As indicated earlier, the Orthodox Church in Greece does not approve of cremation. It is the only church body with an international presence, and with a significant population, that seeks to follow its early Christian ancestors in regard to opposing and rejecting cremation.

Since virtually all Christian denominations have acquiesced to cremation and thus say and do nothing in opposition, it is therefore interesting to note the action the Free Presbyterian Church of Scotland took in 1990 when it opposed a proposed construction of a crematory in Inverness, Scotland. In the church's discussion leading to that decision, one of its clergy stated "that biblical authority supported burial, and that it was a decline in biblical standards that had accompanied the rise of cremation in [Great] Britain."[17]

Regarding the decline of biblical standards that accompany cremation, it is sobering to note that clergy participating in cremation funerals apparently are not bothered by this correlation. Nor do they appear to be bothered using their denomination's old-burial liturgies that are largely incongruous with a cremation funeral. Although funeral liturgies vary from one denomination to another, the *Book of Common Worship* (1993) of the Presbyterian Church (USA) is an example of what an officiating minister is to say as the body is placed into the crematory and later at a columbarium. Cremation is categorically different from earth burial, yet the words of this rite, spoken at the crematory and at the columbarium, are almost identical to those spoken at an earth-burial funeral.[18] This brings to mind the criticism of J. Douglas Davies, theologian and cremationist. Quite appropriately, he has remarked that "most churches have become deeply involved in it [cremation], but they have paid relatively little formal attention to the theological issues involved."[19]

Supposed Biblical Silence

Most people know that the Christian church, apart from the split that occurred in the eleventh century between the Eastern and Western church, and another during the Protestant Reformation in the sixteenth century, today is divided into at least two camps with regard to how the Bible is viewed. One group is the liberal contingent that has been greatly influenced by the historical-critical method of biblical interpretation. It assumes the Bible, similar to other historical documents, is largely the product of fallible men and thus contains errors of fact, judgment, and interpretation. Hence, many statements in the Bible are seen as mere pious opinions expressed as God's Word when they are only expressions of the biblical writers reflecting their personal beliefs or cultural biases. In light of this view, the Bible is not seen as the final source of authority with regard to what may or may not be believed or practiced by members of the church. Thus, when it comes to cremation, for example, what the Bible has to say about it is not really relevant today.

Some of the more prominent liberal denominations that essentially reflect this view of the Bible are the United Church of Christ; the United Methodist Church; Presbyterian Church USA; the Episcopal Church in the United States of America; the Evangelical Lutheran Church in America; the American Baptist Churches in the USA; the Reformed Church of America; and the United Church in Canada. Some smaller denominations could be cited as well.

In contrast to the liberal groups are the conservative denominations. For the most part, they are the Assemblies of God; the Southern Baptist Convention; the Christian Reformed Church in North America; the Mennonite Church USA; the Orthodox Presbyterian Church; the Evangelical Presbyterian Church; the Lutheran Church—Missouri

Synod; the Eastern Orthodox churches in America; the Wisconsin Evangelical Lutheran Synod; the Evangelical Lutheran Synod; and the Wesleyan Methodist churches. Some additional groups could be cited here too.

These latter denominations see the Bible as God's revealed and inspired Word and thus the only guide and rule for Christians in terms of their faith and life. They tend to say if a given behavior or practice is prohibited in the Bible, Christians may not do it. However, when the question arises of whether cremation is biblically permissible, their clergy commonly say the Bible is either silent on the matter or that it does not prohibit it. Some clergy like to use the Latin term *adiaphoron,* meaning a given practice or activity is neither biblically commanded nor forbidden. Thus, these conservative church bodies do not have a different policy in regard to cremation than do liberal churches. In reality, both groups have succumbed to accepting the pagan practice of incinerating the dead.

Thus one cannot assume that because a denomination is conservative it is opposed to cremation. Kenneth Iserson made that faulty conclusion in his informative book *Death to Dust: What Happens to Dead Bodies* (1994). He lists the Lutheran Church—Missouri Synod, an internationally known conservative denomination, as being opposed to cremation.[20] But Iserson was mistaken, for this church body, then and now, is as permissive with regard to cremation as any liberal church body. It even has a rubric in its *Lutheran Service Book Agenda* (2006) relative to conducting a cremation funeral. The rubric reads, "In the case of cremation, the ashes are to be buried or entered at a cemetery plot, mausoleum, crypt, or columbarium."[21]

On the basis of supposed biblical silence, here are some statements of acquiescence on the part of some conservative churches. One example is from the Lutheran Church—Missouri Synod (LCMS). In the "Q & A" section of this synod's official publication, *The Lutheran Witness,* a member asked, "Due to the cost of funerals, my husband and I are considering cremation. Is this considered Christian, and what is the position of The Lutheran Church—Missouri Synod on this matter?" The response said, "Cremation is not forbidden by Scripture and therefore may be considered."[22] In effect, this response says the Bible is silent on the matter of cremation, a statement that ignores Amos 2:1–2, 1 Corinthians 3:16–17 and 6:19–20 and Romans 12:2. It also ignores the fact that cremation is often mentioned in the Old Testament as one way God exercised his wrath (discussed in chapter 3), and it ignores centuries of Christian opposition to cremation, not to mention that when Christians today have themselves cremated, it leads many to conclude that they no longer believe in the resurrection of the body. The latter is reinforced by what J. Douglas Davies has noted. "It might even be argued that cremation services foster disbelief in the resurrection."[23]

Given Davies's comment, it is fair to ask: Are conservative church bodies and their clergy oblivious to his conclusion? Does the fostering of disbelief in the resurrection of the body not disturb them? Do they no longer care whether their members still believe in the resurrection of the body? Are they not bothered that by their accepting cremation they are unwittingly giving support to those who do not believe in the resurrection? The latter concern, as we have seen, was a major reason why the early Christians rejected cremation.

The following are some additional statements from conservative denominations pertaining to cremation. The Southern Baptist Convention (America's largest Protestant denomination) indicates that the Bible is silent on cremation. Its website states, "The act of cremation is not a sin." The website makes this conclusion by contending that it would only be a sin if it violated one of God's laws, and since God has no such law, it is therefore not a sin. Thus the website states, "The disposal of the body is left to our desires and wishes in accordance with the law of the land."[24]

The Wisconsin Evangelical Lutheran Synod (WELS) has stated the following on its website. "God does not say anything in the

Bible about the cremation [sic] of a human body to reveal whether he approves or disapproves of it. Therefore we classify the custom as something God has neither commanded nor forbidden, that is, a matter of Christian freedom."[25]

The conservative Wesleyan Methodist Church also sees the Bible as leaving the matter of cremation to the individual Christian's decision. In a letter addressed to me, one executive of this church body wrote, "The Wesleyan Church has no published statement on cremation one way or the other. Some members use cremation. There is apparently no theological objection to it."[26] Quite similar to this position is the stance of the Mennonite Church USA. One of its officials in a letter quoted a portion of the church's position. It reads, "Memorial services after burial or cremation are common."[27]

In its pamphlet "General Christian Doctrines," The Assemblies of God (Springfield, Missouri) mentions the traditional Christian reservations concerning cremation. But it also lists some extenuating circumstances where cremation may be permitted or even necessary, such as limited land space to bury people and the matter of costly burial plots. It further says, "There is no biblical evidence for thinking a Christian will miss heaven because of cremation."[28]

Apart from many churches that say the Bible is silent regarding cremation, some only speak about cremation in a positive way. For instance, *Reformed Worship,* a periodical of the Christian Reformed Churches in North America recently published an article strongly supportive of cremation, titled "Better than a Cemetery?"[29] It lauded a Presbyterian church's construction of a columbarium. Readers of this article can only conclude that cremation obviously is not forbidden in the Bible. And the periodical, *Christianity Today,* published an article whose author stated, "The Bible should not be used as a proof text either for the necessity of burial or for 'cremation on demand.'"[30]

To Cremate or Not Is Not an Open Question

From the biblical references and their contexts cited earlier, as well as other citations mentioned in chapters 3 and 6, it is evident that cremation is not an open question for Christians. Hence, it appears that clergy and churches who say the Bible is silent regarding whether Christians may or may not opt for cremation either have not really examined the issue biblically, or because of the powerful influences of today's secular culture, they have taken the path of least resistance and conformed to this practice of the secular world.

To tell Christians today that the Bible is silent regarding cremation could only have some credibility if Christian clergy and theologians had done the following: (1) Studied all of biblical references that directly and indirectly pertain to cremation and found those references in light of sound biblical and theological reasoning are truly irrelevant for Christians today; (2) Made a thorough historical study showing that Christians were misguided for nearly two thousand years by their seeing cremation violating their biblical heritage and theological values. Such studies, however, do not exist. Aside from a handful of individual authors who have briefly written for or against cremation, a search of denominational literature reveals not a single denomination has ever produced a biblical, historical study on cremation. To cite J. Douglas Davies once more, "Most churches have become deeply involved in it [cremation], but they have paid relatively little formal attention to theological issues involved."[31]

Given the absence of formal theological studies, it is left up to each individual church member to decide whether cremation may or may not be chosen. This is illustrated by one denomination's official who, upon being asked if his church body had a position on cremation, replied to me in writing, "Individual members of a church ... would have to determine their belief regarding cremation."[32] Here one is reminded of the words in the book of Judges. "Everyone did what was right in his own eyes" (Judges 21:25).

Do Not Conform to This World

Mention has already been made of how the early Christians in Rome seemed to be mindful of St. Paul's command telling them they were not to conform to this world (Romans 12:2). Thus, it is important to note that this command of God's is ignored today when Christians are either told or led to believe that cremation is an acceptable option for them. One cannot help but ask: Why do so many Christian clergy and churches today not see Romans 12:2 applying to the practice of cremation? This is especially puzzling since cremation is pagan in its origins, and St. Paul clearly did not want Christians to conform to pagan practices.

Certainly, the early Christians knew and believed if they imitated the pagan Romans by practicing cremation, they would have conformed to the world of their day. So they refused to conform. We have seen in chapters 4 and 6 from the early-Christian writer Minucius Felix that the Romans despised Christians for not conforming to their pagan custom of cremation.

If the words of Romans 12:2 do not apply to cremation, it is difficult to see to what worldly practice they do apply. Moreover, Christians today do not seem to realize how serious the early Christians were about their not to conforming to the ways of the Roman world. Heeding that biblical admonition also resulted in their rejecting other pagan practices, mentioned earlier. Thus, it seems quite plausible the early Christians' rejection of cremation was not unrelated to St. Paul's words, "Do not be conformed to this world."

It is important to note when Paul told the Christians in Rome not to conform to this world, he did not mean that they were not to wear Roman togas or sandals, or speak Latin. Rather, he had in mind behavior that was morally and theologically significant. By not conforming to the world, Paul wanted Christians to glorify God and rebuke the world's ungodly ways. G. K. Chesterton, the insightful British Christian, once said, "If the world grows too worldly, it can be rebuked by the church, but if the church grows too worldly, it cannot be adequately rebuked for worldliness by the world." Hence, the churches and clergy having accepted cremation—indeed a worldly practice—will certainly not be rebuked by the world for having accepted its values.

Cremation and Cafeteria Theology

In some form or another, virtually all Christian denominations practice what can be called cafeteria theology. They heed and honor only those biblical passages that meet their theological or cultural tastes. Thus, when clergy or theologians say the Bible does not prohibit cremation, one wonders whether it would really make any difference even if the Bible clearly stated, "You shall not cremate yourself or your neighbor."

Given the powerful force of culture, it is not an exaggeration to argue if there were such a proscriptive statement in the Bible, it likely would not change the present-day attitude and practice of those churches that have already accepted cremation. Nor would it be the first time that plain proscriptive statements in the Bible have been ignored. The Bible, for instance, clearly underscores the death penalty in Genesis 9:6 and Romans 13:7 and in other passages, but most of today's clergy, as well as most denominations (Roman Catholic and many Protestant groups) in their opposition to capital punishment have chosen to ignore the Bible's pro-capital punishment passages.

The wide acceptance, or at least toleration, of abortion on demand today by many mainline Protestant churches and their clergy is another example of ignoring what the Bible's clearly states. These churches no longer tell their members that abortion on demand is wrong and sinful. They refuse to apply the biblical commandment, "You shall not murder" (Exodus 20:13) to abortion. And they also ignore the abortion proscription taught in the early church, "You shall not kill a child by abortion" (*Didache* II). Some denominations, via their denominational health insurance policies, even help defray medical costs for their female clergy having abortions on demand.

The biblical condemnation of homosexual behavior, as stated in the Old and New Testament, is also increasingly ignored by many mainline denominations. Some are now even ordaining clergy who are known to be practicing homosexuals. And some denominations have their clergy performing same-sex marriage ceremonies, uniting two homosexual men (or two lesbians) as though they were husband and wife. St. Paul quite clearly warned that practicing homosexuals "will not inherit the kingdom of God" (1 Corinthians 6:9), but this biblical warning is summarily ignored by many church bodies.

Thus, it is at best wishful thinking to argue that if clearly stated biblical passages existed prohibiting cremation, today's churches and their clergy would reject cremation. The secular culture's values and practices, many of which have already been adopted by numerous denominations, will not let biblical prohibitions impede their already prevailing presence, no matter how clear such biblical passages might be.

The Fire of Cremation Vis-à-Vis the Fire of Hell

Jesus clearly taught not only that there was a heaven but also a hell, and that hell was a place of eternal fire. He told his disciples, "It is better for you to enter life crippled or lame than with two hands or two feet to be thrown into the eternal fire" (Matthew 18:8). This fact reveals an unrecognized irony in regard to those Christians who see cremation as an acceptable way to dispose of their dead bodies. Recently, an opponent of cremation asked a rather pointed question: "If these same Christians desire to be saved from the fires of hell by their faith in Christ, then why do they willingly subject themselves to the fires of cremation, similar to what those are experiencing in hell?"

Some Fallacious Pro-Cremation Arguments

In their acquiescing to cremation, some clergy and theologians often put forth some rather specious arguments in defense of their accepting cremation. The following are some examples.

Equating Dust with Ashes

One argument often heard says, given that the interred human body will turn to dust, the cremated ashes are therefore no different than the dust that will result from the body decaying in the grave. It is an old, faulty argument. Caecilius, the Roman pagan and critic of Christianity, in the second century, already made this erroneous argument when he falsely stated Christians thought "each body, if it were spared flames, could not be resolved into dust in the same course of years as by the length of time" (*Octavius* 11). He wrongly equated the ashes of cremation with dust resulting from a body's decay. As indicated earlier, chemically speaking, dust and ashes are not the same.

This faulty equation is sometimes even made by some conservative Christian theologians. For instance, a theology professor, a nonadvocate of cremation, said, "Whether a body returns to dust by the longer process of decomposition or by the shorter process of cremation is immaterial."[33] Similarly, the *New Catholic Encyclopedia* has one of its contributors write, "In itself the end result of cremation is no different from that of natural decomposition."[34] This argument is also used by cremationists who argue cremation really does not differ much from a buried body's final state, except that cremation speeds up the process.

Even if it were true that the speeding-up process turns the cremated body into dust, it would be wrong to do so, according to Donald Howard. He argues, "The dissolution of the body is not a natural process that we are at liberty to hasten or delay at will. It is the punishment which God has inflicted upon sin."[35] Moreover, to justify the speeding-up process is reminiscent to what philosophers call the "naturalistic fallacy," meaning it is a fallacy to appeal to the normality of a given consequence in order to justify the morality or goodness of the consequence.

Fire as a Symbol of "Divine Presence"

Stephen Prothero, a cremationist, says Christians might want to see cremation as acceptable because fire is a symbol of divine presence, as when God presented himself to Moses by speaking to him in a burning bush.[36] Similarly, William E. Phipps, a professor of religion and philosophy, in his book *Cremation Concerns* (1989), says Christians have no real cause to oppose the fire of cremation because the Bible says "God is a consuming fire" (Hebrews 12:29). But this latter reference only conveys divine judgment, devoid of any comfort. Moreover, it is difficult to see how these two biblical references, whose context do not pertain to cremation, can logically be applied to cremation.

With regard to the metaphor of fire, Phipps also contends that Christians should be at ease with cremation because on the first Christian Pentecost the Holy Spirit appeared to the disciples in tongues of fire, and also because the Nicene Creed speaks of this Holy Spirit as the "giver of life."[37] Phipps further argues that Christians should remember that the season of Lent "traditionally ended with lighting a candle during the Easter vigil in recognition of the light of Christ dispelling the world of darkness. Thus, a radiant flame has at least as many holy associations as dark earth."[38] Again, to apply these two biblical references to cremation is contrary to sound hermeneutical logic.

In response to Phipps, the following criticism, made by Norman L. Geisler and Douglas E. Potter, is noteworthy. "While fire in some cases may be seen as good or serve as a symbol of divine presence, it is wrong to apply it to cremation."[39] This criticism shows that in the Bible, "Fire was most often associated with warning and judgment (Leviticus 10:1-2), including eternal judgment (Matthew 25:4, etc.) ... and hell fire itself."[40] Indeed, the Bible also says anyone whose name is not written in the book of life will be "thrown into the lake of fire" (Revelation 20:15). And not to be overlooked are the words Christ spoke concerning his second coming, namely, at that time his angels will cast the lawless "into the fiery furnace" (Matthew 13:42). These biblical references do not provide a wholesome picture of fire.

Erroneous View of the Resurrection

Cremation from the early years of Christianity was seen by pagans as nullifying a dead body's future resurrection. When cremation today fosters this old, mistaken belief in the minds of many, it does not seem to bother many who favor cremation. It seems to matter little or nothing to them whether Jesus raised dead Lazarus from his grave or that God will raise the dead in the future. To cite Phipps again, the raising of Lazarus by Jesus he says is a "weird story."[41] And regarding the future resurrection of the dead, he contends that St. Paul in 1 Corinthians 15:44, where he speaks of the resurrected body being a spiritual body, "does not mean the reassembling and the reanimation of the corpse."[42] Phipps expands on this by saying, "The expression 'spiritual body' which he [Paul] uses does not refer to the physical skeleton and the flesh on it. Rather, in modern terminology, it means the self or the personality."[43] This interpretation is a radical departure from the biblical doctrine of the resurrection, for it implies that Christ's resurrected body, the first-fruit of all resurrections, as Paul called it (1 Corinthians 15:23), was not a physical body. This conclusion is false on several counts.

First, Christ's resurrected body did in fact have real flesh and bones, for he told his disciples, "Touch me, and see; a ghost does not have flesh and bones, as you see I have" (Luke 24:39). And after he spoke these words, he gave his disciples additional evidence by eating some broiled fish in their presence (Luke 24:42–43). Another time, he asked the doubting Thomas to touch the crucified wounds of his resurrected body (John 20:27). This experience prompted Thomas to say, "My Lord and my God" (John 20:28). Clearly, this was a response to Christ's body having physical qualities. It was not an apparition.

Second, Phipps' understanding of the phrase *spiritual body* is wrong, for Paul did not speak about a spiritual body that is nonphysical. The latter is not what the Greek words *soma pneumatikon* (spiritual body) mean in 1 Corinthians 15:44, as N. T. Wright (the renowned British theologian) has definitively shown in his book *The Resurrection of the Son of God* (2003, 347–56). The words *soma pneumatikon,* as Wright states, "is a body animated by the Spirit of the living God, even though only one example of such a body [Christ's] has so far appeared."[44] Biblically anchored Christian theology has always taught that *soma pneumatikon* refers to Christ's post-resurrection body—a glorified body—that is "spiritual, not as to substance, but as to qualities and endowments."[45] Phipps's understanding of "spiritual body" is unequivocally wrong. For Paul spoke about a glorified body, that is, Christ's resurrected body. Note, he says, "it [the body] is raised in glory" (1 Corinthians 15:43), and he further underscored this point in his letter to the Christians in the city of Philippi, where he told them that their bodies on Resurrection Day "will be like his [Christ's] glorious body" (Philippians 3:21).

Misrepresenting an Early Christian Document

In his ardent defense of cremation, Phipps argues that at least one early Christian had no problem with cremation, namely, Minucius Felix who wrote the dialog *Octavius* in about AD 195. In his dialog (cited earlier) the character named Octavius (a Christian) tells the pagan Caecilius that the world will someday be destroyed by fire. And in this context, in which everything would be destroyed, including human bodies, Octavius, the Christian, asks Caecilius,

> Do you think that, if anything is withdrawn from our feeble eyes, it perishes to God? Everyone's body, whether it is dried up into dust, or is dissolved into moisture, or is compressed into ashes, or is attenuated into smoke, is withdrawn from us, but it is reserved for God in the custody of the elements. Nor, as you believe, do we fear any loss from burning, but we adopt the ancient and better custom of burying in the earth. (*Octavius* 34:10)

To be sure, these words show that Octavius and his fellow Christians did not think it impossible for God to resurrect human bodies destroyed by fire, but his words do not condone cremation. Phipps erroneously thinks Octavius's words indicate he and the early Christians had no problem with cremation. He seems to have forgotten that Caecilius earlier in the dialogue had accused and criticized Christians for execrating and condemning Rome's funeral pyres. If it were true that the early Christians had no problems with cremation, then how does one explain Caecilius's accusation?

Phipps further distorts the words of Octavius by referring to the Vatican's approval of cremation in 1963, by saying, "the Roman Catholic church has returned to the outlook of Minucius Felix."[46] In light of the accusation Caecilius made regarding Christians despising cremation, it is simply false to say the church "has returned to the outlook of Minucius Felix." This implies that Octavius and the early church at one time approved of cremation. But there is no historical evidence that any early Christians ever approved of cremation.

Faulty Use of Citing Cremated Christian Martyrs

Another argument sometimes made in support of cremation invokes the martyrdom of early Christians, whom the pagan Romans at times executed and then burned. There are at least two well-known examples. One is Polycarp, the bishop of Symrna, whom the pagans burned at the stake in AD 156. The other is the large number of Christians whom the pagans murdered and then incinerated in Lyons, Gaul (modern France) in AD 177. On the basis of examples as these, it has been argued by some cremationists if cremation prevents God from raising the dead, then he would be punishing those who were his faithful Christian witnesses (martyrs). It is in this context that the words of Lord Shaftsbury (1801–1885), who supported the cremation movement in England in the 1870s, have been cited by cremationists. He asked, "What in such a case would have become of the blessed martyrs?" Shaftsbury's argument, similar to what the pagan Romans believed, erroneously assumed the long-standing opposition to cremation by Christians was based on their believing that cremated bodies could not be resurrected. It was an assumption that had no historical support.

Arguing for Cremation with Wrong Biblical Passages

Still another faulty argument used to support cremation pertains to cremationists citing biblical references that are presented as speaking about cremation when in fact they do not. The American physician Hugo Erichsen, a zealous promoter of cremation in the 1880s, used this deceptive method to promote cremation. In his book *The Cremation of the Dead* (1887), he cites 2 Chronicles 16:14 as evidence that Asa, the king of Judah, was burned on a funeral pyre. The passage he quotes from the King James translation reads, "And they buried him in his own sepulchers, which he had made for himself in the city of David, and laid him in the bed which was filled with sweet odors and divers kinds of spices prepared by the apothecaries' art; *and they made a very great burning of him*"[47] (original emphasis). Erichsen takes license with this passage, for the last two words in the King James translation read "for him," but he changed them to read "of him." No translation, then or now, has ever rendered the words "for him" to read "of him" in this passage. In fact, two renowned Hebrew scholars, C.F. Keil and F. Delitzsch, both contemporaries of Erichsen, in their scholarly commentary show this passage refers to the burning of spices, a common Hebrew practice done in honor of the king. Thus, this reference has nothing to do with cremating King Asa.[48]

Erichsen also cites Isaiah 30:33 in support of the Hebrews cremating deceased persons. This passage in the King James Version reads, "For Topheth [place of abomination] is ordained of old; yea, for the king it is prepared; he hath made it deep and large; the pile thereof is fire and much wood; the breath of the Lord like a stream of brimstone doth kindle it."[49] As many Old Testament scholars have shown, this reference in Isaiah does not refer to cremating deceased bodies, but to "where Israel [sinfully] offered human sacrifices to Molech by fire."[50] The prophet Jeremiah corroborates this by saying, "They have built the high places of Topheth in the Valley of Ben Hinnom to burn their sons and daughters in the fire, something I [God] did not command" (Jeremiah 7:31 KJV). Erichsen cites still another biblical reference from Jeremiah 34:5 in trying to show the Hebrews did at times cremate their dead. This passage also does not say what Erichsen tries to make it say, but rather it states how Zedekiah, the king of Judah, will die and what funeral practices will take place. "But thou shalt die in peace, and with the burnings of thy fathers, the former kings which were before thee, so shall they burn odours for thee" (Jeremiah 34:5 KJV). No recognized Old Testament scholar has ever understood this passage as speaking about a cremation. Instead, it has always been seen referring to the burning of spices at funerals, similar to the passage in 2 Chronicles

16:14, cited above. One scholarly commentary says these words of Jeremiah promise King Zedekiah that his "funeral shall be honored with the same burning of aromatic spices as there was at the funerals of [his] fathers (II Chronicles 16:14; 21:19)."[51]

It is unfortunate when completely false arguments are made in support of any position, whether it is about cremation or some other topic. But it is even more unfortunate when faulty arguments try to make biblical passages say something they clearly do not say. Such arguments, made in support of cremation, obviously confuse, or worse, mislead many uninformed Christians to conclude falsely that there really are acceptable Old Testament precedents for cremating the dead, when in fact there are none.

Churches House Urns and Build Columbaria

One does not have to look long to find churches that today are housing urns of their cremated members. In recent years some churches with larger memberships have even constructed columbaria. These are often specially built church hallways with niches in walls designed to accommodate urns of cremated members. Some churches also have urns located inside of a court-like space adjoining the church's physical structure. Churches with columbaria justify their efforts by saying that the survivors now are able to pay respect to their departed relative(s) every time they attend church by stopping to view the urn(s). Some churches now are also giving the name columbarium a broader meaning by using this term for specially designed plot of ground where urns of members are buried adjacent to the church. The *Reformed Worship,* a periodical (1992), carried an article of one such columbarium.[52] Niches in congregational columbaria that house cremated ashes, of course, are not free or inexpensive. A given niche may sell from $200 to $2,000, depending on the socioeconomic status of the congregation's membership.

Still other churches have members who scatter the ashes of a departed relative among ornamental shrubs adjacent to the church building. Thus, the acquiescence of clergy and churches is not merely confined to accepting cremation. By some churches facilitating the scattering of ashes on church property and housing urns in church columbaria they are helping institutionalize the ideology that underlies the practice of cremation. One cannot help wonder what the early Christians would have said about such ecclesiastical capitulation.

The Economic Argument

Many individuals, including some Christians, choose cremation because they think it is less costly than earth burial. The economic argument, however, is not so simple as is often assumed by people favoring cremation. Many Americans and Canadians still buy caskets when they cremate their deceased relative, and these caskets vary in price, as they do with earth burials. To complicate the cost factor even more, some mourners rent a casket, enabling them to take the body to a church funeral, and then after the funeral service is over they have the body taken to a crematory, where it will be cremated in a firm, less- expensive container. This makes it is difficult to arrive at an average cost for a cremation.

A well-known funeral home in Florida in 2013 charged about $3,500 for a cremation funeral. [53] And according to the National Funeral Directors Association, the average cost of an earth-burial funeral in 2014 ranged between six and eight thousand dollars.[54]

Even when there is a substantial price difference between earth burial and cremation funerals, cost difference should not be an acceptable reason for Christians to choose cremation. Christianity's theological values should outweigh the cost factor. And when the cost differences truly are a factor for some families, then today's Christians should do as the early Christians did by assuming the costs of burying the poor and indigent. In some instances, as Tertullian (church father, d. ca. AD 225) has noted, the early Christians bore the entire costs for burying the poor (*Apologeticus* xxxix).

Conclusion

As already noted and underscored, God does not want Christians to conform to the ways of the world. To the contrary, Christ told his disciples that they were to be "the light of the world" (Matthew 5:14), and they were to let their "light shine before men" (Matthew 5:16). These words do not support today's churches condoning and accepting cremation.

In 1926, before any Christian denomination had capitulated to cremation, Bertram S. Puckle, a renowned scholar of funeral rites, stated that Christians could never accept cremation "without violating the most ancient and sacred traditions of their respective beliefs."[55] Thus, Christian denominations that are now quite comfortable with cremation are clearly violating Christianity's "ancient and sacred traditions of their respective beliefs" every time one of their clergy conducts a cremation funeral.

[1] Frederick S. Paxton, *Christianizing Death: The Creation of the Ritual Process in Early Medieval Europe* (Ithaca, NY: Cornell University Press, 1990), 95.

[2] Patrick Sims-Williams, *Religion and Literature in Western England, 600-800* (New York: Cambridge University Press, 1990), 76.

[3] John Castleman Swinburne-Hanham, "Cremation," *The Encyclopaedia Britannica* (Cambridge, England: At the University Press, 1910), 404.

[4] Hugo Erichsen, *The Cremation of the Dead* (Detroit, MI: D.O. Haynes & Company, 1887), 50.

[5] Ibid.

[6] "Divine Truth," *Vital Speeches* (August 1, 1968), 612.

[7] John Breck, "An Orthodox Perspective on Cremation," in John Breck, *The Sacred Gift of Life: Orthodox Christianity and Bioethics* (Crestwood, NY: St. Vladimir's Seminary Press, 1998), 279.

[8] Ibid., 282.

9   Nicon D. Patrinacos, *A Dictionary of Greek Orthodoxy* (Pleasantville, NY: Hellenic Heritage Publications, 1984), 104.

10   Ibid.

11   Ibid.

12   George Papaioannou, "Cremation vs. Burial Rites," *Orthodox Review* (December, 1988), 5.

13   A letter written to me by Archbishop Mor Cyril Aphrem Karim (January 13, 2003).

14   John Shahovskoy, "The Church and the Cremation Problem," www.holy-trinity.org/morality/shahovskoy-cremation.html. (accessed July 11, 2014).

15   Ibid.

16   Victor Potapov, "Cremation: Earth Thou Art and Unto Earth Shalt Thou Return," www.stjohnde.org/homilie/homcremt.htm.

17   J. Douglas Davies, *Cremation Today and Tomorrow* (Bramcote, England: Grove Books Limited, 1990), 9.

18   *Book of Common Worship* for the Presbyterian Church (USA), (Louisville, KY: Westminster/John Knox Press, 1993), 941.

19   Davies, op. cit., 6.

20   Kenneth V. Iserson, *Death to Dust: What Happens to Dead Bodies?* (Tucson, AZ: Galen Press, 1994), 274.

21   *Lutheran Service Book Agenda* (St. Louis, MO: Concordia Publishing House, 2006), 124.

22   "Q & A, Cremation," *The Lutheran Witness* (July, 2009), 27.

23   Davies, op. cit., 13.

24   Website of the Southern Baptist Convention (January, 2003).

25   www.wels.net (accessed July 11, 2014)

26   This citation is from a letter received in January, 2003, in response to my inquiring what the position on cremation was in the Wesleyan Church.

27   This citation is from a letter received in January 2003, in response to my inquiring what the position on cremation was in the Mennonite Church USA.

28   The Assemblies of God, "General Christian Doctrines," *Perspectives* (Springfield, MO: Office of Public Relations, n.d.), 36–37.

29   Martha Moore, "Better Than A Cemetery?" *Reformed Worship* (June, 1992), 10–11.

30   Timothy George, "Cremation Confusion," *Christianity Today* (May 21, 2002), 66.

31   Davies, op. cit., 6.

32   This statement is in a letter regarding a denominational response to my inquiry about its stand on cremation.

33 John H. C. Fritz, *Pastoral Theology: A Handbook of Scriptural Principles* (St. Louis, MO: Concordia Publishing House, 1932), 307.

34 R. Rutherford/Eds., "Cremation," *New Catholic Encyclopedia* (Detroit, MI: Thomson/Gale in Association with Catholic University of America, 2003), 4:359.

35 Donald Howard, *Burial or Cremation: Does It Matter?* (Carlisle, PA.: The Banner of Truth Trust, 2001), 23.

36 Stephen Prothero, *Purified by Fire: A History of Cremation in America* (Berkeley, CA: University of California Press, 2001), 93.

37 William E. Phipps, *Cremation Concerns* (Springfield, IL: Charles Thomas Publisher, 1989), 55.

38 Ibid.

39 Norman L. Geisler and Douglas E. Potter, "Ashes to Ashes: Is Burial the Only Christian Option?" *Christian Research Journal* (July-September, 1998), 31.

40 Ibid.

41 Phipps, op. cit., 22.

42 Ibid., 55.

43 Ibid.

44 N.T. Wright, *The Resurrection of the Son of God* (Minneapolis, MN: Fortress Press, 2003), 354.

45 Johann Andreas Quenstedt, "Of the Resurrection of the Dead" in Heinrich Schmid, *The Doctrinal Theology of the Evangelical Lutheran Church*, translated and revised by Charles A. Hay and Henry E. Jacobs, 1899 (Minneapolis, MN: Augsburg Publishing House, 1961), 641.

46 Phipps, op. cit., 57.

47 Hugo Erichsen, *The Cremation of the Dead* (Detroit, MI: D.O. Hayes and Company, 1887), 6.

48 C.F. Keil and F. Delitzsch, *Commentary on the Old Testament*, trans. Andrew Harper (Grand Rapids, MN: Eerdmans Publishing Company, 1978), 3:371.

49 Erichsen, op. cit., 6.

50 Robert Jamieson, A.R. Fausset, David Brown, *Commentary: Practical and Explanatory on the Whole Bible* (Grand Rapids, MN: Zondervan Publishing House, 1967), 546.

51 Ibid., 639.

52 Moore, op. cit. 10–11.

53 This figure was given to me in a telephone conversation with the director of the funeral home.

54 This figure was also given to me in a telephone conversation.

55 Bertram S. Puckle, *Funeral Customs: Their Origins and Development* (New York: Frederick A. Stokes Company Publishers, 1926), 226.

CHAPTER 10

CREMATION MISCELLANEA

A habit not resisted soon becomes a necessity.
                                        —St. Augustine

This chapter discusses a number of issues related in various ways to the practice of cremation that have developed in the West since the latter half of the 1800s. In some instances, the issues cited are largely the result of cremation; in other instances, they have contributed to its acceptance and expansion; and in still other cases, they are complementary to it.

Secularism and Cremation: A Direct Correlation

It is quite obvious the dramatic increases in cremation rates noted in chapter 1 are directly related to the growing impact of secularism. Secularism's influence on Western culture, for example, is apparent in the noteworthy decline in biblical, moral values and practices. In the 1970s abortion on demand became legal in many Western countries, including the United States in 1973. Thus, from 1973 to 2012 some fifty-five million unborn babies in the United States were executed in their mothers' wombs.[1] In the mid–1990s, partial-birth abortion in the United States had increased in popularity. This resulted in the death of 2,200 babies per year from the mid–1990s to 2003, according to the Alan Gutmacher Institute's report in 2003.[2]

Another example of moral decline pertains to family living. The rate of sexual cohabitation among unmarried couples has increased dramatically the past fifty years. In 1960, the American rate of unmarried cohabitation, for instance, was 0.4 million, but by 2011 the rate had risen to 7.6 million.[3] And the divorce rate had almost doubled from 1965 to 1994.[4] In addition, the United States has had a phenomenal increase in out-of-wedlock birth rates during the last forty years. In the mid-1960s, about 5 percent of all American births occurred out of wedlock, but by 2010 the figure had catapulted to 40.8 percent. The out-of-wedlock birth rate for black Americans in 2010 was 73 percent, and among white Americans it was 33.2 percent.[5]

Whether it is abortion on demand, nonmarital cohabitation, high divorce rates, upwardly spiraling out-of-wedlock birth rates, they are all indicators of today's entrenched secularism, a cultural phenomenon in which biblical/Christian values by an increasing number of Westerners are being minimized, ignored, or even rejected. Given the pervasive presence of the current culture's secularism, it is not unrealistic to argue that secularism has in the last fifty years also greatly contributed to the rapid increase in cremation rates that now include a significant number who call themselves Christians. Today, many Christians no longer accept some of the basic biblical doctrines of Christianity, once held by their parents, grandparents, and their Christian ancestors centuries ago. Thus, Christians who now see cremation as an acceptable option have become a part of today's secular cultural syndrome.

In 2006, the Barna Research Group in a national survey found 59 percent of Americans who identified themselves as "evangelical" did not believe their dead bodies would ever be resurrected. And in 2009, Barna discovered that only 62 percent of born-again Christians in the United States believed Jesus lived a sinless life; thus 38 percent did not. Barna also found only 46 percent of born-again Christians believed in moral absolutes.[6]

To see the powerful impact secular culture has had on American Christians, for instance, over the last several decades, it is helpful to compare Barna's findings with a nationwide study published in 1965 by Charles Glock and Rodney Stark in their book *Religion and Society in Tension*. Their study asked whether American Christians believed "Jesus is the Divine Son of God and I have no doubts about it." They found 69 percent of the Protestants and 86 percent of the Catholics said yes.[7] While this question by Glock and Stark is not exactly the same as asking whether Jesus lived a sinless life, it is similar. That said, we see a tremendous secular shift away from traditional-Christian beliefs since the mid-1960s relative to what Christians today believe about the divinity of Jesus Christ. For almost two thousand years it was unheard that any Christian did not believe Christ lived a sinless life. But in 2009, as noted above, only 62 percent of born-again-American Christians believed Christ lived a sinless life.

Glock and Stark also asked whether the miracles recorded in the Bible "actually happened just as the Bible says they did." They found that 57 percent of the Protestants and 74 percent of the Roman Catholics answered yes.[8] Although the question Glock and Stark asked is not quite the same as asked by the Barna researchers, one can argue that if people say they believe miracles actually happened as reported in the Bible, it can be assumed that in their minds the Bible is therefore "totally accurate" in terms of the question Barna asked. Thus, when we compare Barna's current findings with the earlier Glock and Stark data, we see that now only 34 percent of the Protestants and 26 percent of the Catholics believe the Bible is totally accurate. Again, we see a major shift away from traditional Christian beliefs to a secular orientation that has occurred among those who for some reason still consider themselves Christian.

The impact of secularism, as reflected by the decline in the biblical beliefs of American Christians from the mid-1960s to the present time, helps explain why cremation rates have increased

900 percent from the mid-1960s to 2010. Sociologists have used rising abortion rates, out-of-wedlock birth rates, declining beliefs in traditional Christian doctrines, and rising divorce rates as indictors of secularism. Now they have an additional indicator: rising cremation rates.

Secularism's influence, measured by the decline in biblical beliefs, brings to mind the words of the British historian Paul Johnson. He argues that Western society is engaged in pseudo-religion as it opts for "Christianity without Christ [that] tends to leave out the obligatory element in either conduct or beliefs."[9] Thus, given the direct correlation between secularism and cremation, the following question seems appropriate. Will this correlation stir the consciences of the clergy and their churches to take an in-depth-biblical look at cremation in terms of its impact on the church? That, however, is not likely to happen because the clergy too have absorbed much of their culture's entrenched secularism.

Has the Churches' Acceptance of Cremation Weakened Their Gospel Message?

Although the process of secularization has undoubtedly contributed to the capitulation of clergy and churches regarding cremation (discussed in chapter 9), the question also arises whether their capitulation has affected or weakened other parts of the church's message. Since most churches and their leaders no longer believe cremation to be wrong or unbiblical, about which Christians for almost two thousand years did not have the slightest doubt, it does not seem too speculative to think many church members may now conclude that some other Christian beliefs and practices need no longer be accepted either. If the latter is true, the rejection or ignoring of Christianity's longstanding opposition to cremation by today's clergy and churches may be affecting some other Christian beliefs and thus weaken people's conviction regarding them, too.

In short, how much has secularism that has influenced churches to accept cremation encouraged people, for example, also to reject the belief that Christ lived a sinless life, to not see premarital cohabitation as sinful, to accept abortion on demand, and to no longer see homosexual behavior as sinful? Although we do not know how much the acquiescence to cremation on the part of clergy and their churches has contributed to numerous Christians no longer accepting these moral/ Christian positions, it does not appear to be an irrelevant question.

"Land Is for the Living"

The advocates and defenders of cremation argue that earth burial in cemeteries wastes land. Cremation would help solve this problem. Hence, they cry, "Land is for the living." Not so long ago, a publication of the Roman Catholic church gave support to this argument when it asserted that cremation might be a good option for Catholics, because "land especially in metropolitan areas, has become limited" (*The Catholic Yearbook,* 1998).

True, land is for the living, but can one authoritatively say that it is not also for the dead? When God himself practiced earth burial by burying Moses (Deuteronomy 34:6), and when he commanded that criminals be buried (Deuteronomy 21:23), he also gave land to the dead. When the economy of land argument arises, it needs to be remembered that of the estimated two million acres of land currently used in the United States for cemeteries, not all of these acres are suitable for cultivation and raising of crops or for other productive purposes. Many cemeteries are on hillsides that are not suitable for arable use. Thus, Christians in defense of the biblical practice of earth burial should encourage the use of more hillsides or other terrain that has little or no agricultural value when additional cemetery space is needed.

The concern voiced by pro-cremationists about using valuable land space for cemeteries is rather a selective argument and loses much of its credibility when it is carefully considered. Their argument overlooks or ignores the vast amount of land that is consumed by the proliferating number of golf courses, particularly in recent years. In fact, many advocates of cremation who argue against the use of cemetery land space are likely also avid golfers.

Cremation: A Cultural Revolution[10]

In the 1960s and '70s, Communist China, under Chairman Mao Tse Tung, engaged in a culture revolution designed to remove all traditional cultural values and symbols and replace them with Marxist ideology and symbols. China's culture revolution was radical. For that matter, any culture revolution is radical because it tears up traditional, highly treasured, and long-held values and practices of an existing culture. Similarly, cremation is doing this to the cultural values and practices that for centuries have been associated with earth burial.

As documented earlier, cremation in the minds of many is undermining the biblical doctrine of the body's future resurrection. The current rising rates of cremation are making it extremely difficult for biblically minded Christians to resist being influenced or affected by the old pagan argument that cremation means there can be no resurrection of the body. In a funeral service where Christians used to see the deceased person in a casket, it was a lot easier for them to visualize that this deceased person—and someday they too—would be bodily resurrected. But in a cremation service there is no casket and no body. Thus, if during such a service, reference is made to the body's future resurrection, if it is still mentioned today, it will likely be seen as a theological anomaly.

To Christians earth burial has always been a symbolic reminder that the departed person, whom they saw lying in a casket and then lowered into the grave, was "asleep" and would someday rise from the dead. But with cremation the person's body no longer exists. It has been destroyed. It has been turned into ashes that increasingly are scattered somewhere on land or on a body of water. Hence, there is no grave, no grave stone, and no tomb that serves as a reminder of the person who once lived among his or her fellow Christians. Thus, cremation is indeed a cultural revolution, at least in the Western world, because for nearly two millennia earth burial was an integral part of Western culture. Burying the dead notably distinguished the West from the non-Christian Orient, where for centuries cremation has been the cultural norm. But now cremation is destroying this longstanding, significant component of Western culture.

People Desensitized

During the last four decades, at least in the United States, since abortion on demand was legalized by the country's highest court in 1973, the secular mass media have usually cast a positive light on abortion that Christians for centuries saw as contra-biblical, as immoral, and as murder. But when a given phenomenon has been legal for a long time (from 1973–2015) and practiced by so many, namely, abortion on demand, countless people, even those who know abortion is an evil act, eventually become desensitized to it. Culture, as a powerful force, has a way of desensitizing people to behavior and activities that once were accepted as wrong and immoral.

With regard to cremation, it appears that many Christians, similar to abortion, have also become desensitized. The destructive flames of violence and other effects, once seen as cruel and unthinkable, now appear to be increasingly taken in stride, and even seen as economically prudent. In the past, when Westerners witnessed open-air cremations, it was not uncommon for them to ask bystanders, "Could you do this to your mother or father?" They were sensitive to the horrors of burning a human body. But now, given that cremations are done in modern crematories—out of sight to the survivors—the fire of violence to which the deceased body is exposed is no longer visible. And as more and more cremations are taking place, people are slowly becoming desensitized to its violent, destructive nature. (Here the reader may recall the dead body's reaction in cremation described earlier in chapter 3.)

Catastrophic Fires and Other Conflagrations

Some individuals defend cremating humans by comparing it to catastrophic fires, for instance, such as volcanoes, spacecraft disasters, or the thousands who perished in the massive conflagration when the Twin Towers of the World Trade Center in New York City on September 11, 2001, went up in flames, killing and incinerating nearly three thousand individuals. Defenders of cremation say if we can accept or live with the results of such a calamity, we should also be able to accept cremation for conventional deaths.

This is a flawed argument. First, what has happened, whether it is the result of natural forces, human accidents, or disasters beyond human control, does not mean we may imitate such phenomena by cremating deceased human beings. This way of arguing is what philosophers call the "is-ought fallacy" (a.k.a., the naturalistic fallacy), namely, because something happens or exists, it therefore ought to be. Second, this argument implies that when a natural calamity occurs, God willed it. Thus, it is argued, if God permitted fire in a natural calamity to destroy human beings, it cannot be wrong for us to cremate our dead relatives or friends. This reasoning, of course, ignores the difference between what God wills and what he permits. And even when God does will something to happen, it is notably different from what we may do. Third, the argument also ignores the fact that even when God willed or commanded the destruction of given human beings by fire in the Old Testament, it was done as a form of divine punishment.

Living in a precarious and unpredictable world, it is possible that I, who am firmly convinced that people who have themselves cremated are acting contrary to God's will, could someday be killed and burned to death in some flaming conflagration. If that were to happen, I have no doubt that my dead, incinerated body will be resurrected at Christ's second coming. But a body burned in a conflagration may not be compared to bodies destroyed in today's crematories. In the latter instance, the body's unburned bones are ground up, whereas in the former instance the bones are still present, thus making it possible to bury them. This is an important distinction that cremationists fail to make when they equate bodies burned in some infernal disaster with what happens in modern crematories.

Memorial Services: Have They Made Cremation More Acceptable?

The funeral industry uses the terms *immediate cremation* or *direct cremation* when the corpse is cremated before the funeral service takes place in either a church or in a funeral chapel. Thus, there may or may not be an urn with *ashes* present during the funeral ceremony following the body's immediate cremation. In some instances, cremation takes place after the funeral ceremony, and so the body may be present in the church or in the funeral chapel before it is cremated.

When a funeral, however, has no urn present, it has much in common with what we call a "memorial service," where there also is no body present because the person in most instances has already received a conventional burial or was cremated. Since the body of the deceased is not present at a memorial service, it prompts one to ask: Have memorial services unwittingly helped pave the way for today's growing acceptance of cremation? An affirmative response to this question seems likely.

Sociologically speaking, many social activities commonly have unintended consequences and often with negative effects. Memorial services have not helped people remember the significance of why Christians through the centuries had the deceased body present in a church's funeral service. As one insightful observer has noted, "It is the body and not just the remains that is honored during the funeral liturgy in the church."[11]

Regarding memorial and cremation funerals, one keen observer has recently remarked, "Curiously, we [North Americans] are rapidly becoming the first society in the history of the world for whom the dead are no longer required—or desired—at their own funerals."[12] Given this common custom today, this same observer asked, "Why do we memorialize the dead by banning them from our presence?"[13] Understanding today's culture, he then answered his own question. "We don't have the body, and much of the time, we don't want to have the body."[14]

Earth Burial and Expensive Caskets

When Jessica Mitford's book *The American Way of Death* first appeared in 1963, it caused a national stir by exposing the expensive and extravagant mortuary practices that were often the result of pressuring grieving mourners who were frequently urged to do "the best" for their departed loved one. What Mitford observed can still be seem in many American and Canadian funerals today. Family mourners, stricken with sorrowful emotions, and not wanting to feel guilty, often buy highly expensive hardwood (walnut, oak, cherry) caskets and other costly, needless items. One estimate indicates that each year more 200 million pounds of steel are used to manufacture caskets.[15] Unfortunately, caskets often serve as social status symbols. Some mourners even purchase caskets furnished with inner spring mattresses for the corpse to lie on. Many American mourners think they have to spend liberally on their loved one's funeral because it is the last thing they can do to show their love for him or her. Ironically, the deceased person is not the one who sees this so-called gesture of love.

Although I have consistently defended earth burial in the present book because it is the biblically approved way of laying deceased persons to rest, I do not want anyone to conclude that earth burials must be expensive and extravagant. The lowest-priced casket can suffice, and no Christian should feel guilty or "cheap" for buying the least-costly casket and other related low-cost items. Parents would probably do their children a big favor if they in advance requested, both in a formal will and also in personal conversations that they desired to have the least-expensive casket, with no frills of any kind. Moreover, since there are no American state laws requiring individuals be buried in hardwood or steel caskets or concrete vaults, no Christian would be amiss if he or she even asked to be buried in a plain pine box that can be acquired without much difficulty. And given such a request, survivors should not let their perceptions of what others might think influence them to ignore what the deceased member had requested. Here it might be helpful if Christians knew that until about the mid-1800s, Christians were not buried in coffins. These came into use "when elaborate funerals demanded time for their preparation."[16]

By opting for an unelaborate, inexpensive funeral today's Christians may benefit from knowing the attitudes that prevailed among the church fathers in the early church. Frank Senn correctly shows, "The church fathers inveighed against rich grave clothes and sumptuous trappings, and recommended instead a simple shroud and the giving of alms."[17]

Interestingly, funeral expenditures for caskets are not limited to earth burials. Many individuals who are cremated are inserted into the crematory's furnace in a casket, especially those whose bodies are incinerated after the funeral service has already taken place. Often, the caskets used in cremations are as costly as those used in earth burials. Although most crematories do not require caskets, they do require the corpse to be encased in a firm container. No crematory in the United States or Canada will incinerate a corpse wrapped only in a body bag.

Denying Death

For some time some social analysts have been saying Westerners have created a death-denial culture, a phenomenon evident in several ways. When, for example, a family member is not cremated in the United States or Canada, the survivors want him or her to look nice, almost lifelike, in the casket, an effect produced by embalming. People are pleased when the mortician was able cosmetically to make a person in the casket look virtually as good as when he or she was alive. In addition, it is not uncommon to hear people, after they have viewed an embalmed body, say that the deceased "looked really good." Here we have an unrecognized example of denying death.

Death is also denied, at least linguistically, by the common expression people utter when someone dies. Instead of saying a given person has died, we hear people say the person has "passed away." This expression also has a variant form: "We mourn his passing." Both expressions apparently are prompted by an unrecognized socio-psychological need to deny that death has occurred when someone has died. It should also be noted that the expression *passed away* is really incompatible with the Christian concept of the death as sleep, and it is also at odds with the early-Christian custom of referring to a Christian's day of death as *dies natalis* (day of birth). Death, as previously stated, was for the early Christians "the day of birth into eternity, a time of joy."[18]

To be sure, people know that the expression, *passed away* or *passing,* refers to someone having died. But what is not really recognized is that our secular culture has succeeded in getting people to say someone has died without actually saying so. It is our culture's way of denying the reality of death, and most people who utter these expressions seem quite unaware of what they are saying culturally when they utter either of these two expressions. The following paragraph sheds additional light on the death-denial phenomenon.

In "The Pornography of Death" Geoffery Gorer in 1955 argued that in England "belief in the future life as taught in Christian doctrine is very uncommon today even in the minority who make church-going or prayer a consistent part of their lives; and without some such belief natural death and physical decomposition have become too horrible to contemplate or discuss."[19] A decade later in his book *Death, Grief, and Mourning* (1965), he showed that death in Western societies had become a taboo, and one way people coped with this taboo was to deny the reality of death as much as possible.

Interestingly, there is a certain amount of reciprocity between a death-denial culture and cremation. Cremation supports people's denying death by sparing them from seeing a dead body at a funeral. Even when an urn is present at a funeral, either at the church or at the mortuary, the experience is substantially less emotional than seeing a deceased person lying in a casket. On the other hand, the culture that denies death helps promote cremation because of the psychological benefits it imparts to those who unknowingly deny the reality of death. The latter has undoubtedly contributed to the rapid rise in cremation rates since the 1960s.

Recently, another phenomenon is beginning to become part of the West's death-denying culture. Some funeral directors now are offering services providing various settings that reflect a key interest or hobby the deceased person had or valued in life. If the deceased was an avid basketball fan, the funeral director has the mourners sit around a basketball hoop next to the casket; if the individual loved outdoor grilling, a grill and its accessories are the focus of attention, together with the aroma of corn roasted on the cob; and if the person, say, a woman, greatly enjoyed baking, an oven with fresh loaves of bread and cakes perched on or beside a stove will be located near the casket in a mortuary.

A manager of a mortuary that provides these special services said, "It's not like you're at a funeral home; it's like you're at home. It makes it just a happy place to be. No one has said, 'That's creepy.'"[20] Given some of these funeral activities, Craig Parton has noted that funerals in our culture today are becoming "fun-erals."[21] And Joe Queenan, in his book, *Balsamic Dreams: A Short But Self-Important History of the Baby Boomer Generation* (2001), sees these new funeral services as "transform[ing] the traditional funeral service into a ludicrous stage show."[22] He goes on to say: "Funerals are no longer somber rituals where we pay our respects to the dead. They are cabaret."[23] Queenan might also have added that these services, which he sees as a product of the Boomer Generation, are the most recent examples of a death-denial culture, and perhaps that is what he has in mind when he says, "It is no secret that Baby Boomers have a hard time dealing with death."[24] The latter, however, seems to have preceded the Boomers by at least a generation if Geoffery Gorer's *Death, Grief, and Mourning* (1965) analysis is correct.

Clergy Redundancy?

In light of the high cremation rates in the UK (74 percent of all deaths in 2010), J. Douglas Davies wonders whether the clergy might not someday become redundant (superfluous) as the result of increased secularization of funeral practices. His British research findings published in 1990 reveal "there is the possibility of about 25 percent of the [British] population being content with people other than clergy conducting funeral rites."[25] In 2002, a dozen years after Davies' findings, an article in *The Church Times* of London, England, reported that "civil funerals" (in which clergy do not participate) backed by the government, would be held in April 2002 in seven areas of the country.[26] Civil servants provide information for this type of funeral to the survivors when the death of the deceased is registered. Officiants at these funerals are known as "civil registrars."[27] The article noted that church leaders expressed concern about these funerals because they lack pastoral care and also cost about twice what clergy receive, and undertakers saw them invading their turf.

While I am not aware of any research data regarding the percentage of Americans who feel comfortable with someone other than clergy conducting funeral rites, it does not seem unrealistic to envision that since the increase in cremation rates is related to the process of secularization, clergy might someday in the minds of many no longer appear necessary or even desirable, especially at cremation funerals. If this were to happen, it would indeed be an irony because pro-cremationists would not be returning the favor that the clergy extended to them when they accepted their cremation ideology and practices.

Apart from cremation, the redundancy of clergy is already a reality at many North American funerals. This phenomenon is not really recognized because pastors and priests still officiate at the majority of funerals. The redundancy, however, is evidenced by the major roles relatives of the deceased person often assume when they determine what musical selections, regardless of the lyrics, and other elements of the funeral service will be used. Numerous church members, many of them with only a nominal membership status and poorly versed in Christian doctrine, select funeral songs completely devoid of any Christian hope and faith. "Wind Beneath My Wings," "Forever Young," and "In the Garden" are some common examples. Songs like these make no mention of the redemptive work of Jesus Christ or to a future resurrection of the body. This omission is usually not recognized by family members of the deceased, and they are likely to get upset when they are told their selections conflict with basic Christian doctrine because it usually means little or nothing to them. Moreover, the sentimental appeal of their selected songs is the only thing that matters, and when clergy acquiesce to their demands, they are in effect fostering clergy redundancy.

What about Christians Already Cremated?

Devout Christians reading this book, which on the basis of biblical evidence and centuries of earth burials by Christians has shown that cremation is not a God-pleasing practice, may wonder and ask: "What about my Christian spouse or relative who was cremated?" The Christian who asks this question is obviously concerned and should receive a pastoral answer. Such an answer should assure the person that although God nowhere approves of cremation in the Bible, we must remember that he is all powerful, and that he can indeed resurrect any cremated human being. In this context, it would also be well to remind the person that because God in his omnipotence can resurrect cremated bodies, it does not mean Christians have his permission to cremate additional deceased bodies.

If a Christian feels guilty about having been a part of the decision to cremate a spouse, a relative, or a friend, assurance should be given that God through his Son Jesus Christ forgives this sin just as he forgives any other sin upon repentance and trust in his forgiveness. In this context, it would also be appropriate for a pastor to remind the concerned person of the assuring words Christ spoke to the adulterous woman: "Go and sin no more" (John 8:11).

Conclusion

This book was not written to indict individual Christians if they have been part of a pro-cremation decision but rather to show them biblically and theologically that cremation, contrary to what most Christian denominations say and do today, does not have God's approval. I wrote this book to encourage Christians not to conform to this world as St. Paul had asked the early Christians (Romans 12:2), and that they would continue to bury their dead, as their Christian ancestors did for almost two thousand years. Christians must not in ignorance bring back and honor an age-old pagan practice that symbolically detracts and casts doubt in the minds of many on the cardinal doctrine of Christianity, the future resurrection of the body.

Biblically speaking, cremation is not a matter of one's choosing. As James Fraser, a Christian pastor, has stated, "Burial is the only

God-given way of honorably disposing of the dead."[28] His following words are even more noteworthy, as he asks: "Is cremation Christian? Positively no! It is of heathen origin … a barbarous act, also antibiblical and therefore, *unchristian!* [sic]."[29]

---

[1] Minnesota Citizens Concerned for Life (www.mccl.org/us-unborn-stats. html), accessed on October 2, 2012.

[2] In 2003, the United States passed the Partial-Birth Abortion Ban Act. In 2007, the United States Supreme Court upheld the constitutionality of this law.

[3] The US Census Bureau, 2011, as reported in *The Journal of Marriage and Family* (August, 2012), 794.

[4] *Statistical Abstract of the United States: 2001* (Washington, DC: U. S. Department of Commerce, 2001), 51.

[5] National Vital Statistics Reports (August, 2012), furnished by US Department of Health and Human Services.

[6] "Worldview Among Christians," *Barna Research Group* (March 6, 2009).

[7] Charles Y. Glock and Rodney Stark, *Religion and Society in Tension* (Chicago: Rand McNally and Company, 1965), 93.

[8] Ibid., 96.

[9] Paul Johnson, *Enemies of Society* (New York: Atheneum, 1977), 120.

[10] H. Richard Rutherford, a Roman Catholic priest who is not opposed to cremation, uses the term *cultural revolution* relative to Americans increasingly opting for cremation. I am indebted to him for this term relative to the popularity of cremation. See his "Forum: Cremation American Style: A Cultural Revolution for Catholics," *Worship* (November, 1992), 544–49.

[11] H. Richard Rutherford, "Honoring the Dead: Catholics and Cremation," *Worship* (November, 1990), 486.

[12] Thomas G. Long, "Habeas Corpus . . . Not," in Thomas G. Long and Thomas Lynch, *The Good Funeral: Death, Grief, and the Community of Care* (Louisville, KY: Westminster John Knox Press, 2013), 93.

[13] Ibid., 96.

[14] Ibid., 94.

[15] Kenneth V. Iserson, *Death to Dust: What Happens to Dead Bodies?* (Tucson, AZ: Galen Press Limited, 1994), 468.

[16] J. Morley, *Death, Heaven and the Victorians* (London: Studio Vista, 1971), 96.

[17] Frank Senn, *Christian Liturgy: Catholic and Evangelical* (Minneapolis, MN: Fortress Press, 1997), 166.

18 Jon Davies, *Death, Burial and the Rebirth in the Religions of Antiquity* (New York: Routledge, 1999), 196.

19 Geoffery Gorer, "The Pornography of Death," *Encounter* (October, 1955), 51.

20 Jim Suhr, "Not So Somber Send-Off," (www.cbsnews.com/stories/2002/10/31).

21 Craig Parton, "Funerals From Hell: Where Have All The Graveyards Gone?" *Modern Reformation* (January–February, 2010), 6.

22 Joe Queenan, *Balsamic Dreams: A Short But Self-Important History of the Baby Boomer Generation* (New York: Henry Holt and Company, 2001), 97.

23 Ibid.

24 Ibid.

25 J. Douglas Davies, *Cremation Today and Tomorrow* (Bramcote, England: Grove Books Limited, 1990), 18.

26 Rachel Harden, "Burials Without the Benefit of Clergy," *The Church Times* (London, February 15, 2002).

27 Ibid.

28 James Fraser, *Cremation: Is It Christian?* (Neptune, NJ: Loizeaux Brothers, 1985), 13.

29 Ibid., 20.

CHAPTER 11

CHURCHES AND CLERGY ACQUIESCED TO FUNERAL DIRECTORS

A little neglect may breed great mischief.
—Benjamin Franklin

Until the mid-1800s, Americans cared for their dead in the confines of their own homes. But by the time of the Civil War in the early 1860s organized funeral directing in the United States slowly made its appearance. Then in 1882, some morticians and undertakers founded the National Funeral Directors Association (NFDA).

Funeral Directors and Funeral Homes

Roughly two decades after the NFDA's founding, the organization urged its members to promote themselves as professionals rather than tradesmen often known as casket makers. For many years, preparing deceased bodies for burial by undertakers was not a solitary business but one often combined with another business, for instance, a carpentry shop, an upholstery shop, or even a hardware store. With the growth and urbanization of the United States, the undertaking business slowly became more common and more popular. This made it financially feasible for business-minded undertakers to operate a mortuary not associated with some other business venture.

The NFDA was quite successful in getting the public to see morticians and undertakers as professionals, and in time it was also successful in getting the public to go along with its funeral practices, for instance, embalming (discussed in chapter 12). Briefly stated, funeral directors have had an immense influence on American and Canadian culture, an influence that has shaped people's attitudes concerning funeral practices.

Funeral Services in Mortuaries

In addition to churches and clergy having acquiesced to accepting cremation, they have also acquiesced to another current practice. They now often conduct funeral services in a mortuary chapel rather than in the church of the deceased member. This is a major departure from what Christians did for centuries.

By World War II an increasing number of church members, Americans and Canadians, were having their funeral services conducted in a mortuary chapel. Here too this appears to be a direct correlation between secularization and the increase in funeral services conducted outside the confines of a church building.

It is difficult to determine whether this practice was first promoted by the funeral directors or whether the directors filled a need that had occurred because many church members with no close ties to their churches chose to have the funeral service of a deceased relative conducted in a funeral home. It may be that both parties contributed to this present-day practice.

Even if both parties in tandem brought about the funerary services in funeral homes, there is another contributing factor that has and continues to play an important role supporting these services conducted in mortuary chapels, and that is the uncritical acceptance of this practice by the clergy and churches. It is apparent that many Christians, including their pastors or priests, no longer deem it theologically important to have funeral services held in the church.

They seem not to be aware that when a departed person's family opts to have the funeral service held in a funeral home, rather than in church, a silent message is conveyed to the public, including to Christians. Knowingly or unknowingly, that message says the church likely was not an important factor in the deceased person's life. And when pastors or priests fail to encourage (and many are) dying members to have their funeral services conducted in the church, they are supporting their culture's growing secular beliefs and values, rather than those of the Christian church.

When a funeral service is held in a church, with the deceased person's body present, it conveys an important message that says his or her life was anchored in Christ and that the church building was an important place in that person's life. It also conveys a testimony that the deceased person understood the Psalmist's words. "Lord, I love the habitation of your house and the place where your glory dwells" (Psalm 26:8). And it further tells the funeral's attendants, "If we live, we live to the Lord, and if we die, we die to the Lord. So whether we live or die, we belong to the Lord" (Romans 14:8).

From a Christian perspective, conducting a service in a funeral home also reveals another discomforting fact. Architecturally, mortuary chapels are devoid of all Christian symbols. The design and furnishings of the typical chapel with no Christian symbols makes non-Christians more comfortable than committed, informed Christians who commonly would be spiritually comforted if a cross and an altar were present. The typical mortuary chapel is essentially designed to accommodate agnostics, atheists, Unitarians, and other non-Christians, more so than Christians. The absence of Christian symbols also means a conscientious Christian pastor cannot reinforce the funeral service's homily with any relevant symbols. Particularly affected are liturgical churches, for the interior of their churches provide an environment of Christian symbols that remind survivors and friends of the deceased person's Christian faith, but in mortuary chapels Christian symbols are conspicuously nonexistent, thus depriving mourning Christians of salutary spiritual benefits.

There is also a problem regarding Christian music. If a pastor and the family of the deceased person desire to have a couple of recorded hymns played in the mortuary's chapel—if any are available—they will invariably be nonlyrical selections "piped in" via an audio system. And if the request is for Christian hymns with lyrics in order to accent the departed person's faith in the resurrection of the body, the response will usually be that the chapel does not have such hymns on hand.

In light of how secular culture has led clergy and church members to accept the funeral industry's way of conducting funerals services today in mortuary chapels, one wonders whether either one is even aware that they have acquiesced to a completely non-Christian funeral setting. Moreover, when some pastors are aware of the situation, they now have little or no choice, for if they declined to "go along to get along," they would likely lose their positions because they would probably receive no support from their denomination's leaders for their noncompliance.

In view of this current phenomenon, the question arises, why or how did the funeral industry attain such prominent influence and authority? How much of this phenomenon is the result of many church members having been only nominally involved in the life of their churches? How much of it is the result of Christians and their clergy having become secularized? And how much of it is the result of clergy not having taught their members why they should desire to have their funerals conducted in a Christian church?

Ushering Mourners Away from the Grave

Churches and their clergy have capitulated to another relatively recent funeral practice. For centuries, Christian family members and their mourning friends, standing at the grave side, would gently toss a handful of earth on the casket after it had been lowered into the grave. By gently tossing some soil, the mourners reminded themselves of the words God spoke to Adam soon after he had fallen into sin, "Dust you are and to dust you will return" (Genesis 3:19). Most traditional committal liturgies contained a specific rubric indicating at what point in the ceremony mourners could toss soil onto the lowered casket. In the past, family members and their mourning friends commonly sang a hymn, just before the pallbearers shoveled the earth back to fill in the grave. But today, after the committal words are spoken by a pastor or priest, the funeral director commonly ushers all mourners away from the grave, preventing them from tossing some soil onto the casket, from singing a hymn at the graveside, from seeing the casket lowered into the grave, and finally from seeing the grave filled in.

Since the current practice of ushering mourners away from the grave before it is filled in preempts a centuries-old Christian custom, it raises an important question. Is this practice really beneficial to the mourners? Some say no. They contend spiritually and psychologically this honorable custom helped those who grieved obtain final closure by seeing the casket lowered into the grave and closed with God's good earth.

Ushering mourners away from the grave before the casket is lowered and the grave closed brings to mind some recent reports that have revealed some irregularities in regard to the burial of dead bodies. One report (March 2002) indicated that individuals sometimes are not buried where they were supposedly buried, and that sometimes two bodies are interred where only one was to be buried.[1] Hence, if family mourners were permitted to stay at the graveside until the grave is closed, they would have no reason later to wonder whether their loved one is really resting in the grave where they initially saw him or her buried.

The current custom of funeral directors ushering mourners away from the grave, and thus preventing them from seeing the actual burial completed, is not without some consternation on the part of some groups. For example, Jay Miller, an anthropologist, reports that some American Indians, upon attending "Anglo burials are often shocked when the family walks away from the grave with the coffin still resting above it."[2] Miller also notes: "All Native [sic] funerals I have ever attended end with the family lowering the coffin and filling in the grave, often with separate lines of men or of women tossing handfuls of soil into the grave to soften the later impact of loaded shovelfuls."[3]

Funeral directors have become accustomed to having activities go their way. Thus, many directors not only prevent mourners from seeing the closing of the deceased person's grave, but some now even place the soil from the grave in storage nearby and later bring it back to fill in the grave when the mourners are gone. Whether mourners requested this service or whether funeral directors unilaterally introduced it is difficult to determine. If the latter is true, it is another example of Christians and the clergy having capitulated to funeral directors. Thus, as one critic has rightly stated, Christian churches no longer have the privilege in "shaping and presiding over the rites of death."[4]

Conclusion

In spite of St. Paul's words that urge Christians not to conform to the values and practices of the world, as has been noted a number of times in this book, so many Christians nevertheless do conform to the world. This was seen again in the present chapter that showed how Christians capitulated to the funeral industry's present-day practices. Given that these practices are relatively new in the history of funerary activities, Christians have not had the background to inform themselves with regard to the accompanying theological problems concerning these practices. Thus, this chapter's discussion of today's funeral practices vis-à-vis Christian theological values was not written to indict pastors or churches but to alert them to funerary problems not readily recognized today, given that today's secular culture easily preempts and camouflages important Christian values and practices.

---

[1]   Kit R. Roane, "Burial Plots: Cemetery Abuses Mean Your Loved Ones May Not Be Resting Where You Think," *U.S. News and World Report* (March 11, 2002), 22.

[2]   Jay Miller, "Ashes Ethereal: Cremation in the Americas," *American Indian Culture and Research Journal* (2001), 133.

[3]   Ibid.

[4]   Paul P. J. Sheppy, *Death Liturgy and Ritual: A Pastoral and Liturgical Theology* (Burlington, VT: Ashgate Publishing Company, 2003), 8.

CHAPTER 12

EMBALMING:
IS IT BIBLICALLY CORRECT?

> *Appearances often are deceiving.*
>
> —Aesop

> *Nothing is more powerful than custom.*
>
> —Ovid

The previous chapters focused on Christianity's rejection of the pagan Roman practice of cremation. Those chapters did not discuss embalming the dead, but not because the Romans in the early years of Christianity did not bury any of their dead. They did indeed bury some, primarily those from the lower socio-economic status who could not afford cremation that required a large amount of costly cypress wood. The Romans also did not bury most of the indigent and the culturally undesirables. These were commonly discarded in ditches or, as noted in chapter 8, unceremoniously thrown into the *puticuli* (uncovered burial pits). Clearly, no one embalmed them. Among the few Romans who were embalmed was Poppaea, the wife of Emperor Nero. Reportedly, she died from him having kicked her pregnant abdomen. Along with embalming her in the Egyptian-like manner, her body was stuffed with spices. And Nero gave her an expensive, ostentatious state funeral and publicly displayed her body while he delivered the eulogy.[1]

In addition to Poppaea, the historically renowned Cleopatra and Antony were also embalmed/mummified, and so was the wife of Flavius Abascantus, secretary of Emperor Domitian.[2] However, even after the Romans had abandoned cremation in the fourth century, they, unlike the Egyptians, did not widely practice embalming. Similarly, the early Christians in Rome did not embalm their dead. Here too they followed their Hebrew ancestors, who buried their deceased without embalming them. The Old Testament records only two embalmed individuals, namely Jacob and later his son Joseph, both in Egypt.

Ancient Egyptian Embalming

Jacob had lived in Egypt as an immigrant from Canaan. His son Joseph, a high-ranking official in Egypt, had invited his father, his brothers, and their families to migrate to Egypt to escape Canaan's severe seven-year drought and famine. Later, when Jacob died, his son Joseph ordered physicians to embalm his father (Genesis 50:2). And still later, when Joseph died, he was also embalmed (Genesis 50:26). Given that Joseph had his father embalmed/mummified and later his own body indicates Joseph had adopted Egypt's cultural custom of embalming, quite apart from what his Hebrew ancestors had ever done, for there is no other instance of embalming mentioned in the entire Old Testament. In short, Joseph had no biblical support or approval for what he had the embalmers do to his father and later to himself.

The Hebrews in the Old Testament, as discussed earlier, had a high regard for the human body, even in its deceased state. Thus, did Joseph violate this value his Hebrew ancestors had for the human body when he had his father embalmed and later also himself? This question seems appropriate given what we know about Egyptian embalming from the report by Herodotus (fourth century BC Greek historian). He indicates the Egyptian embalming/mummification process was grotesquely macabre. It consisted of pulling out the deceased person's brains with hooks and removing the intestines and filling the eviscerated abdomen with myrrh and spices. The entire process took seventy days.[3] Other accounts reveal the embalmers filled the emptied skull with resin and cured it for about forty days; next, they anointed the body with perfume and filled the abdomen with herbs or sawdust, and then it was wrapped in linen and placed in a casket for burial, or sometimes it was placed on a couch in a survivor's home.[4] Egyptians of the lower classes were not embalmed or mummified.

Was Jacob's Body Mummified?

Genesis 50:3–4 states that after the seventy days of embalming and mourning for Jacob were over, Joseph asked Pharaoh for permission to transport Jacob's body back to Canaan. Pharaoh granted Joseph's request. This indicates Jacob was not only embalmed but also mummified, for a deceased body merely embalmed without mummification would have badly decomposed and produced an unbearable odor, a phenomenon Joseph and his entourage would not have been able to tolerate on their long journey to Canaan.

St. Antony's Christian Response to Egyptian Embalming

Earlier, in chapter 6 we saw that St. Antony (AD 251–356), the renowned Christian monk in Egypt and reputed founder of monasticism, firmly opposed the Egyptian practice of embalming/ mummifying the dead, even for the socially eminent. To his consternation, he found some deviant Christians in Egypt who, like the pagans, also mummified some of their dead humans, "especially those of the holy martyrs."[5] One historian states that Antony "had always evinced the greatest hostility towards the Christian custom of mummification and keeping the bodies of the dead embalmed for the inspection of relatives and friends."[6] Athanasius, the biographer of St. Antony, quotes him telling Christians, "This practice [embalmment] is neither lawful nor in any way godly, for even the remains of patriarchs and prophets are preserved in tombs to this day. Even the body of the Lord himself was placed in a tomb."[7]

Interestingly, Athanasius wrote, "Yet Antony, knowing their practice and afraid that they would do the same with his body, shared his plans with the monks on the outer mountain and then hastened away ... and after a few months he became ill."[8] However, before he died, he had told two companion monks, "Think about these things yourselves and reflect on them, and if you care about me and keep my memory as you would a father's, do not allow anyone to take my body to Egypt lest they keep it in their homes."[9] He continued, "You know that I have always put to shame those who do this [mummify] and how I have ordered them to stop practices of this sort. Therefore, you yourselves bury me and hide my body under the earth and follow my instructions so that no one knows the burial site except you alone."[10]

When Antony died, his two companion monks faithfully followed his orders, as they "wrapped his body and prepared it for burial and hid it under the earth."[11] And Athanasius wrote, "To this day no one knows where it is hidden except those two alone."[12]

Christians in Egypt Vis-à-Vis Christians in Rome

The early Christians in Rome not only rejected the practice of cremation, but they also did not embalm their dead. However, in Egypt, some Christians (evidently a minority) adopted the pagan custom of embalming—really mummifying—some of their dead, especially those they considered Christian martyrs. Their having done so prompts the question, why?

We know that one prominent reason why Christians in Rome rejected cremation was their seeing the human body as God's sacred creation, whether alive or dead. It was part of their biblical, Judaic heritage. They did not want the body destroyed by fire because it was God's handiwork. They saw it as "fearfully and wonderfully made" (Psalm 139:14). Hence, did certain Christians in Egypt see embalming/mummification as still honoring the body, even though the Egyptian practice removed the body's brains and internal organs? Or did they ignore the biblical view of the human body? Perhaps, but as we have seen, that was not how St. Antony saw it. To him embalmment/mummification clashed with what the Old Testament's patriarchs and prophets did with their dead, and it also ignored that Jesus' crucified body had been buried without embalmment. Anthony wanted Christians buried without any bodily mutilation.

St. Antony's admonishing Christians not to embalm/mummify their dead did yield some results. For Athanasius says, "Many people hid [buried] their dead under the earth and from that time on gave thanks to the Lord, having been taught well."[13] Athanasius, however, did not say that all Christians heeded Antony's admonishments. Undoubtedly, he knew that many did not. And even after Antony's time, some Egyptian Christians, as Philip David Scott-Moncrieff has shown, were still mummifying many of their dead at the time of the Arab (Islamic) conquest of Egypt in 641.[14] They did so in Egypt's regions of Antinoe, Deir-bahari, Akhmin, and the Oasis of Kharga.[15]

Clearly, by embalming and mummifying their dead, some Christians in Egypt, unlike their counterparts in Rome, were less faithful in retaining their Judaic ancestors' practice of burying the dead without embalming them. Interestingly, in spite of the fact that some Christians practiced this Egyptian custom, some historians credit Christianity for bringing an end to mummification in Egypt. Hence, A. J. Spencer writes, "The spread of the new religion [Christianity] dealt the final blow to the continuance of ancient Egyptian funerary practices."[16] Similarly, Jessica Mitford in her book *The American Way of Death* (1998) says Christianity helped bring about the end of mummifying in Egypt.[17] These conclusions, however, are questionable, given that some Christians in Egypt, as noted above, continued to engage in the practice at least for several centuries after St. Antony had commanded them to cease doing so. Moreover, there seems to be no historical evidence that shows Christians were a factor in ending this mortuary practice in Egypt, and it needs to be noted that neither Spencer nor Mitford provide any documentation for their crediting Christians with the demise of Egypt's mummifying practice.

Embalming the Dead Today

Before the American Civil War (1861–1865), embalming in the United States was a rare phenomenon. People saw it as tampering with the integrity of the human body, and it "provoked outrage and horror among antebellum Protestants."[18] But when President Lincoln's body was embalmed, enabling thousands to view him as his funeral train took him from Washington, DC, to Springfield, Illinois, the practice of embalming soon gained wide social acceptance. "Up to this point in time, Americans had largely opposed the idea of embalming. To a mostly American-Christian population, embalming represented a pagan Egyptian practice that involved the grotesque mutilation of the body, a kind of desecration of the human temple of God that was condemned in the New Testament."[19]

When a high-status person is positively associated with a practice that is culturally unacceptable, as was true in the case of President Lincoln, it often gains social acceptance. This shows that the high social status of individuals often functions as a powerful force of social change. It reminds one of Queen Victoria having requested chloroform in 1847 to alleviate her pain in childbirth. Previous to her request, even physicians had opposed its use, but after the queen requested it, not only the physicians but also the public soon accepted it.[20]

However, one cannot help but wonder whether the public would have so readily accepted embalming, even after Lincoln had been embalmed, had it known what had been done to his body by the embalmers. *The Pittsburg Daily Post* reported, "There is now no blood in the body; it has been drained by the jugular vein ... The scalp has been removed [and then replaced], the brain scooped out ... All this we see of Abraham Lincoln, so cunningly contemplated in this splendid coffin, is a mere shell, an effigy, a sculpture."[21] The public did not know what embalming had done to him, and neither does it really know today what embalming does to a deceased body. In this regard, little has changed since Lincoln's day.

Following the embalmment of Lincoln, embalming the dead in the United States soon became more frequent and widespread. Thus, today many Americans, even in some rural areas, call a mortician to get the body and have it embalmed. Interestingly, the acceptance of embalming in the United States also soon appealed to Canada. Hence, when Americans and Canadians today do not choose cremation, they invariably opt for embalming their loved ones or themselves. Most North Americans who do not favor cremation see embalming as an unquestioned necessity, even though it is not legally required.[22] They have unwittingly helped establish embalming "that [has] become so entrenched, so routinized, in fact, that most families believe it is all but required when the death comes calling."[23] Thus, in the United States and Canada embalming is the life-blood of the funeral industry.

North Americans embalm their dead because that is what everyone else does. This brings to mind the words of the Roman poet Ovid, cited above, "Nothing is more powerful than custom."

Embalming Briefly Described

Given that chapter 4 gave a brief description of how the furnace (retort) incinerates the human body, it seems also fitting to give a brief description of what takes place in the embalming room. While it is not pleasant to describe the procedure, it may help individuals, especially Christians, decide whether they someday really want to have their dead bodies physically mutilated and impregnated with extremely toxic, carcinogenic chemicals.

In the first step of embalming, morticians stretch out the body on a stainless steel or porcelain table, and next they wash the body with a germicidal solution. To prevent leakage, morticians stuff formaldehyde-soaked cotton into the anus and the vagina when it is a woman. Morticians usually insert eye-caps under the eyelids, sealed with a cream or glue to keep them from opening. They tie the jaws together by sewing the bottom jaw to the top one; the mouth is made to look normal by using a mouth former that is held in place by applying some cream; the lips are kept together with ointment or superglue; and the mouth is filled with cotton. Next, the jugular vein is cut, along with cutting the carotid artery on the right side of the neck. Then the mortician inserts tubes into these blood vessels, forcing the blood out with a pump that also replaces the blood with embalming fluid that consists largely of formaldehyde, usually pink in color. The pink fluid gives the face and hands a quasi–natural appearance. The drained blood is flushed into the city's or town's sewage system.

Then there is one more major procedure. This one requires making another incision, this one just above the navel, where the mortician stabs a trocar (a spear-like-steel tube) into the dead person's abdomen. Attached to the trocar is a hose leading to a pump that siphons the fluids and gases from the dead body's internal organs (liver, lungs, bladder, intestines, stomach, and abdominal cavity). The embalmer using the trocar stands on a "stool to work the trocar, spearing it in and out … until the [corpse's] belly drops."[24] The extracted fluids, similar to the extracted blood, go into the sewage system. After the entire suction process is completed, the body's cavities in the torso are filled with about two gallons of embalming chemicals. Next, the incision by the navel is closed with a "trocar plug" before the corpse is finally dressed and groomed. On average, the entire embalmment process takes about two to three hours.[25]

The above account indicates embalming mutilates and eviscerates the deceased person's body, a process that treats the extracted contents as waste material, similar to other waste in society. The entire embalming process treats the deceased person as a dehumanized object. One mortician expressed it this way. "Once I've seen a body that is it. I don't treat them [sic] as if that was once a living person. To me … It's just a shell."[26]

Hazardous Nature of Embalming Fluids

In chapter 4, we saw that crematories emit a great deal of pollution, mercury being one of the most prominent. In many instances, the amount of mercury spewed into the air exceeds the environmentally permissible levels set by states or cities. However, what is less well known by the public is the fact that the embalming fluids are also devastatingly harmful to the environment and ultimately to people's health and well-being. One recent report states, "Currently, nearly one million gallons of formaldehyde are buried in embalmed bodies each year in the United States, most of which will eventually seep; into the groundwater and surface waters."[27] And in the 1990s arsenic has been found in well water near some cemeteries in Iowa where Civil War soldiers, embalmed with arsenic, are buried.[28]

The public also does not know that the Occupational Safety and Health Administration (OSHA) requires every embalmer to wear a respirator and full-body covering while engaged in embalming. Nor is it widely known that formaldehyde ("formalin") used in embalming is highly carcinogenic. Curiously, this embalming "effluent is not regulated, and its waste is flushed into the common sewer system or septic tank."[29] Moreover, on November 20, 2009, the *Journal of the National Cancer Institute* published findings online that showed the death rate for myeloid leukemia among embalmers exposed to formaldehyde increased statistically significantly with the number of years employed as embalmers. These findings, in addition to reasons cited earlier, should move every citizen, especially Christians, to seriously question embalmment when his or her time comes to leave this world. Just as cremation is not for Christians, neither is embalmment.

Embalming Provides No Public Health Benefits

Funeral directors tend to tell mourning families that embalming is necessary to protect them and the public from possible diseases, especially if they want a public viewing of the body. This is one of today's most widespread myths perpetuated by many funeral directors. It is a myth uncritically accepted by the public. The Centers for Disease Control (CDC) in the United States and a similar organization in Canada have shown that viewing an unembalmed dead body does not expose viewers to any contagious disease, no more so than sitting in a public bus, sitting in an airplane, or attending some public event. The "CDC has never prescribed embalming as a public health measure [and] it's a scientific fact that dead bodies do not pose a health risk to anyone except in very rare cases."[30] Still, a recent (2007) study found 66 percent of the American public thought that embalming was required by state health law "if the body was not immediately buried."[31]

Anyone desiring a nonembalmment funeral can easily find a mortuary that will honor such a request. Most up-to-date mortuaries have facilities enabling them to refrigerate the body before the funeral takes place, and the cost is considerably less than for embalming. Compliant mortuaries also permit private viewing of the deceased person for the mourning family. Burying unembalmed bodies, of course, is nothing new. Christians buried their dead in this manner for centuries. Moreover, Christians buried their loved ones without a coffin or casket; they respectfully wrapped the body in fine linen or in other suitable material and lowered it into the grave. Today, when one reads about "green burials" (promoted by some environmentally conscious individuals), it is helpful to remember that these burials are similar to what Christians did before coffins or caskets and embalming became common, especially in North America.[32]

The Real Reason for Embalming

Embalming only preserves the body for a very brief period. Once buried, it soon decomposes. Thus, there is only one reason for embalming, namely, to make the deceased person look cosmetically appealing to surviving relatives and other viewers. Briefly stated, embalming mostly serves a socio-psychological need that morticians have persuaded most Americans and Canadians to accept as necessary for a modern funeral.

The public does not seem to know that embalming is not required for health reasons and that it is not legally required. Most North Americans have accepted embalming without a second thought, largely because that is what their friends and acquaintances did when they had a death in their family. In short, embalming is the result of unexamined social conformity, writ large in North American culture.

To be sure, anyone who makes funeral plans and thoughtfully decides not to be embalmed when his or her time to leave this vale of tears will likely be seen as a social deviant in the negative sense. Surviving family members may even feel socially embarrassed. The cultural norm for embalming in the United States and Canada is very powerful, and given that not many individuals want to be cultural deviants, they conform to the embalming mentality. Here, however, Christians need to recall and imitate the courage and steadfastness of the early Christians who rejected cremation against great odds. They were cultural deviants by not conforming to the Roman world's values and customs. Similarly, Christians can follow their example by not conforming to the secular culture's custom of embalming the dead.

Embalming Depersonalized and Professionalized Death

For centuries, humans dying and the disposal of the dead was mostly a family matter. There was no embalming, and there was no mortician or undertaker. Someone in the family usually washed and dressed the deceased, commonly done by a female family member. The body of the deceased would ordinarily remain in the person's home from one to three days, permitting friends and neighbors to come by to see the deceased and to extend condolences.

I still recall my paternal grandfather's death in the 1940s in his home in rural Western Canada and his wife (my grandmother) dressing him. After they ordered a casket, it arrived at the nearest train station. From there two of his sons brought it home, and then they gently laid their father into the casket. No mortician or funeral director was present. Three days later, the family buried him in the church's cemetery, as the pallbearers closed the grave with shovels, while family and friends looked on, singing an appropriate Christian hymn. Today, as noted in chapter 11, mourners and friends are often ushered away by the funeral director from the grave before it is filled in, and a Christian hymn is no longer sung either.

As funeral directors succeeded in giving the impression that embalming is hygienically advantageous to the mourners and the public—contrary to scientific evidence—along with their ushering mourners away from the grave before it is closed, they have not only depersonalized death but also professionalized it. Theirs is a silent message that says they know what they are doing and that their activities are best for the immediate mourners, often called "clients."

The professionalization of today's death and dying is also evident in that morticians have succeeded in getting the public to refer to them as *funeral directors*. Related to this title, a mortuary is now a *funeral home,* a misnomer, for the word *home* implies a permanent residence. To be sure, these new terms sound professional. Moreover, these terms receive social reinforcement by virtue of attractive buildings and shining motor hearses parked by the mortuary. Interestingly, Christians, especially in the United States and Canada, have accepted this professional facade, contrary to what their spiritual ancestors did in caring for and disposing of their fellow departed saints for almost two millennia before the present era.

Embalmment Underscores the Denial of Death

In regard to the effects of embalming, Gary Laderman's observation is worthy of note. He has argued that embalming for many Americans after 1900 "enables them to look at the face of death and not be confronted with the gruesome details of decomposition and decay, or to be worried about the liminal status of the body before its final exit."[33] He further states the embalmers made it possible that mourners and viewers "could create their own personal meanings and memories to counteract the pain caused by death."[34] Briefly stated, embalming contributes to a death-denial mentality. This phenomenon, even apart from embalming, as noted earlier in regard to cremation, is especially common in the United States and Canada, as Jessica Mitford has documented in her book, *The American Way of Death Revisited* (1998).

Embalming: A Way of Honoring the Dead

The consistent opposition and rejection Christians maintained with respect to cremation from the first century to mid-1900s did not hold true for embalmment, at least not for long. In spite of St. Antony's proscription, some Christians as early as the mid-fourth century embalmed and sometimes mummified some dignitaries to honor them. Thus, Constantine the Great, the first Christian emperor, who died in AD 337, appears to have been the first dignitary to be embalmed. Similarly, Emperor Gratian (assassinated in AD 376), also a Christian emperor, was embalmed as well. Admirers of Charlemagne the Great, emperor of the Holy Roman Empire (died in AD 814), mummified and seated him in an upright position wearing his imperial robe. In 1087, William the Conqueror was embalmed, and so was the notorious King Henry VIII in 1547, to name only a few.

Some Christian monks embalmed/mummified some fellow monks. The Capuchins, for instance, "dehydrate[d] bodies by sealing them in chambers for six months, bathing the bodies in aromatic herbs and vinegar, and then exposing them to the sun."[35] Archaeologists have found eight thousand mummified bodies of holy men and some lay individuals in the Capuchin monastery in Palermo in Rome.[36]

Given that the early Christians did not want to desecrate a human body, even when dead, prompts an important question: Why did some monks embalm/mummify some individuals? The best answer to this question appears to be the comment made by Charles A. Bradford. In his book, *Heart Burial* (1933), he states that as "churches were built over tombs of martyrs and their altars hallowed with relics, they [some Christians] came to look at things in a new perspective."[37] This comment also sheds light why some Christians embalmed/ mummified given dignitaries. They too saw things from a new perspective, but they had no biblical support for doing so.

Christians Buried Their Dead Unembalmed

Apart from embalming some emperors, kings, monks, and occasionally some other noteworthy persons, most Christians for centuries did not embalm their dead. Instead, they commonly wrapped the unembalmed body in linen cloth or in some other acceptable wrap and laid it to rest in a grave without a coffin.

Coffins first came into use in the latter-half of the 1800s, and then, primarily in the United States.[38] They facilitated transporting dead soldiers to their homes in different states during the American Civil War (1861–1865). These soldiers were embalmed. Then, after President Lincoln was also embalmed in 1865, embalming became more widely accepted, even though many American Christians considered it desecrating the body. But similar to cremation, clergy and theologians never produced a theological evaluation of the practice. So in the absence of any real opposition, it soon became an unquestioned, culturally institutionalized practice. Thus, when a person today requests a nonembalmment funeral, he or she will likely be considered eccentric. Culturally conditioned relatives, friends, and acquaintances expect to see an embalmed body at a funeral, regardless of that their Christian ancestors did when they buried their dead without embalmment.

Cultural conditioning, unrecognized by most individuals, also stifles curiosity, and so people do not think to ask what embalming does to the body. If they are Christians, they have also failed to ask whether it pleases God to have a divinely created human body subjected to the desecrating process of embalmment. In a vague sense people know that morticians do some embalming, but few, if any, ask what embalming actually entails. They are quite comfortable conforming to their culture's acceptance of it.

North America's Geographic Spread of Embalmment

Embalming the dead entered Canada from the United States by way of Charles Bolton who, before migrating to Toronto, Ontario, had served as a bugler in the Union Army in the American Civil War. Later, in Toronto he established a mortuary and introduced embalming to Canadians who, similar to Americans, soon embraced it. During the Civil War, Bolton was a student of Dr. Thomas H. Holmes, a captain in the medical corps of the Union Army. Holmes became famous for his embalming fallen soldiers during the Civil War and especially so after he had embalmed President Lincoln. Embalmers see him as the "Father of Modern Embalming." He boasted having embalmed 4,028 bodies.[39] Later, while living in Brooklyn, New York, he experimented with different fluids for embalming while he also made and sold root beer.[40] In his final years, he reportedly suffered from insanity, possibly the effect of arsenic he had used in his numerous embalming activities. And most interestingly, although known as the Father of Modern Embalming, before he died in 1900, he reportedly had requested not to be embalmed.

In recent years, the embalming of deceased Americans and Canadians has been declining, but not because they do not like what embalmment does to the human body, but because they are now increasingly opting for cremation. And concerning the latter, they are also largely uninformed.

Conclusion

Apart from the embalming of Jacob and Joseph, which had no biblical support, the Hebrews while in Egypt for four hundred years did not embalm their dead. Nor did they bring the practice with them after their Exodus had taken them from Egypt to Canaan, the Promised Land. They continued to bury their dead, unembalmed, as Abraham the patriarch did when he had acquired land to bury his wife Sarah and later for his own burial. Similarly, when Christians in Rome rejected cremation, they also followed their Hebrew ancestors by burying their dead without embalming them.

Finally, as noted at the end of chapter 10 in regard to cremation, I did not write this book to indict Christians who in the past had arranged for a cremation funeral for a family member but to show them that cremation is not a God-pleasing act or biblically compatible so that they would not do it again. Similarly, the present chapter also does not intend to indict Christians, if they at one time were party to embalming. Rather, I wrote this chapter so Christians might know that their society's culture often has them engage in certain activities that are not compatible with what God wants his people to do. As noted earlier, God wants his people to heed St. Paul's words about not conforming to the world's secular practices, as stated in Romans 12:2. But these words urging Christians not to conform are easily forgotten or ignored, and sometimes many Christians do not even know they are in the Bible. Still, conscientious Christians who in ignorance have in the past made a pro-embalmment decision can take comfort as God's people that in the future they can take a new tack by opting for nonembalmment, for themselves and for their deceased relatives. And doing so, they can comfort themselves with the words of Sabine Baring-Gould's well-known hymn, "Onward Christian Soldiers."

Like a mighty army moves the Church of God;

Brothers, we are treading where the saints have trod.

---

1 See Derek B. Counts, *"Regum Externorum Consuetudine:* The Nature and Function of Embalming in Rome," *Classical Antiquity* (October, 1996), 193.

2 Ludwig Friedlander, *Roman Life and Manners Under the Early Empire*, trans. J.H. Freese (London: George Routledge and Sons, 1913), 212.

3 Herodotus, Book II: 86.

4 "Everything You Ever Wanted to Know about Embalming," http://embalming.net (accessed March 14, 2014).

5 Athanasius, *The Life of Antony*, trans. Tim Vivian and Apostolos N. Athanassakis (Kalamazoo: Cistercian Publications, 2003), 249.

6 Philip David Scott-Moncrieff, *Paganism and Christianity in Egypt* (Cambridge at the University Press, 1913), 206.

7 Athanasius, op. cit., 249.

8 Ibid., 251.

9 Ibid., 253.

10 Ibid.

11 Ibid., 255.

12 Ibid.

13   Ibid., 249.

14   Scott-Moncrieff, op. cit., 102.

15   Ibid.

16   A. J. Spencer, *Death in Ancient Egypt* (New York: Penguin Books, 1982), 193–94.

17   Jessica Mitford, *The American Way of Death Revisited* (New York: Alfred A. Knopf, 1998), 144.

18   Gary Laderman, *The Sacred Remains: American Attitudes Toward Death, 1799– 1883* (New Have: Yale University Press, 1996),16.

19   Mark Harris, *Grave Matters* (New York: Scribner, 2007), 45.

20   Howard W. Haggard, *Devils, Drugs, and Doctors* (New York: Harper and Brothers, 1929), 117.

21   *Pittsburgh Daily Post,* April 22, 1865, 2. Cited in Laderman, op. cit., 159.

22   In the United States embalmment is only required legally when a deceased body is transported across state lines in a public vehicle.

23   Harris, op. cit., 47.

24   Tom Jokinen, *Curtains: Adventures of an Undertaker in Training* (Cambridge, MA: Da Capo Press, 2010), 55–56.

25   Readers who desire more details concerning embalming may consult chapter 1 in "The Embalming of Jenny Johnson," in Mark Harris, *Grave Matters* (New York: Scribner, 2008), 7–29. There are also informative articles on the Internet.

26   Cited in Glennys Howarth, *Last Rites: The Work of the Modern Funeral Director* (Amityville, NY: Baywood Publishing Company, 1996), 73.

27   "Celebrating the Lives of Those We Love," http://celebratelives.wordpress. com/celebration-of-life/embalming/ (accessed April 28, 2014).

28   Harris, op. cit., 39.

29   "Embalming: What You Should Know," http://funerals.org/frequently-asked-questions/funeral-arrangements/48-what-you-should-know-about-embalming (accessed April 28, 2014).

30   Joshua Slocum and Lisa Carlson, *Final Rights: Reclaiming the American Way of Death* (Hinesburg, VT.: Upper Access, Inc., Book Publishers, 2011), 63.

31   Ibid., 58.

32   The "green burial" phenomenon began in 1993 in the United Kingdom and is gaining some acceptance in the United States and Canada. Narrowly defined, a green burial requires that the person buried is not embalmed, no vaulted grave, a bio-degradable coffin, and usually no gravestone.

33   Laderman, op. cit., 174.

34   Ibid. The death-denial effect of embalming that Laderman notes it had on northern Protestants, it can be argued, had similar effects on American Catholics.

35   Christine Quigley, *The Corpse: A History* (London: McFarland and Company Publishers, 1996), 264.

36   Ibid.

37   Charles A. Bradford, *Heart Burial* (London: George Allen and Unwin, 1933), 5.

38   Margaret M. Coffin, *Death in Early America* (Nashville, TN: Thomas Nelson, Incorporated Publishers, 1976), 101.

39   Quigley, op. cit., 55.

40   Coffin, op. cit., 81.

CHAPTER 13

WHAT CHRISTIANS ARE NOT TAUGHT OR TOLD

My people are destroyed for lack of knowledge.

—Hosea 4:6

As noted in the preceding chapters, Christians from their earliest years in Rome and to the early eighteenth century maintained a consistent anticremation posture. So firm was the Christian opposition to cremation that church councils saw no need to issue canons that spoke against it. This is an amazing fact. But by the early eighteenth century the solidarity of Christianity's rejection of cremation had clearly weakened. The church's leaders apparently no longer taught or told Christians why their spiritual ancestors had rejected cremation. Thus, as noted earlier, in 1710 a Mrs. John Pratt in Ireland made the first breach in Christianity's anticremation wall by having herself cremated. Christianity's weakened position was further evident in that Pratt's cremation brought no response from the church's leaders. Nor did its leaders respond regarding some other cremations that occurred later (mid-1800s) in different parts in Europe. In both instances, the church's leaders not only failed to respond, but they also failed to give Christians any historical and theological facts why Christians had always rejected cremation.

Facts Not Taught or Told about Cremation

In my contact with numerous Christians during the last decade, it has become obvious that today's Christians know very little about Christianity's centuries-old rejection of cremation and why Christians consistently took that stance. If today's Christians knew these historical facts, not only would they be spiritually edified but also quite likely not opt to have themselves cremated when their time comes to meet their Maker. Thus, Christian teachers, pastors, priests, and theologians need to teach church members the following facts, and, by doing so, they would be performing a God-pleasing service. The following facts are abbreviated and culled from the book's preceding chapters. They are not cited to indict the church's leaders but to provide assistance to teachers, clergy, and theologians who do not support the current, increasing practice of cremation and who would appreciate having these facts available for teaching, counselling, and discussion.

1. The early Christians knew cremation was a pagan practice that underscored pagan values. It was thus one of several reasons why they rejected cremation.
2. They also rejected cremation because they desired to be buried as Christ had been buried.
3. In the early years of Christianity in Rome, Christians were sometimes persecuted by the pagan Romans for spurning cremation.
4. The early Christians execrated and condemned the Roman funeral pyres, a fact documented in the late second-century dialog known as *Octavius,* authored by the Christian lawyer Minucius Felix.
5. For centuries, Christian opposition to cremation was so pronounced that when pagans converted to Christianity,

they were required to abandon and promise never to choose cremation. It was a condition of membership.

6. Not a single act of cremation in the Old Testament ever had God's blessings.

7. Many cremations in the Old Testament often were the result of God's wrath.

8. Most individuals in the Old Testament who were cremated had either violated God's law(s) or had engaged in some criminal behavior.

9. God in the Old Testament did not tolerate cremation, not even those done by pagans, as indicated in Amos 2:1-2.

10. According to 1 Corinthians 3:16 and I Corinthians 6:19-20, St. Paul taught that every living Christian's body was the temple of God's Holy Spirit. That body, although dead, Christians could not bring themselves to burning and destroying it as though it were mere waste material, an act they saw as sacrilegious.

11. Recent research shows cremation is contributing to the erroneous, pagan belief now held by many Christians who think only the soul survives after death, and that there will be no resurrection of the body.

12. Research also reveals cremation is contributing to the West's denial of death, a phenomenon reinforced by no deceased body present at many cremation funerals of Christians.

13. Christians who opt for cremation unwittingly ignore St. Paul's teaching in I Corinthians 8:13 that admonishes Christians not to spiritually offend other Christians by their given behavior.

14. The pagan Romans stopped cremating their deceased humans in the fourth century, largely the result of Christianity's influence. Thus, earth burial became the only acceptable way to dispose of the dead in the West and remained such for nearly two thousand years.

15. Earth burial became Christianity's first culturally institutionalized norm and practice in the West and continued so for nearly two thousand years.

16. It was not until the mid–1800s that earth burial was formally questioned by organized groups in the West. They also conducted some cremations in different parts of Europe.

17. Cremation with its ashes contradicts the biblical concept of death as "sleep," taught in the Old Testament (Daniel 12:2) and in the New Testament (1 Thessalonians 4:13). Cremated ashes cannot be envisioned as being asleep.

18. The words "ashes to ashes" in the committal phrase "Earth to Earth, Ashes to Ashes, Dust to Dust," often spoken at funerals, are not biblically derived. The Bible never speaks about dead human bodies turning to ashes. It only states that bodies will turn to dust (Genesis 3:19).

19. The early Christians replaced the Greek word *necropolis* (burial site of the dead) with the word *koimeterion* for Greek speakers and *coemeterium* for Latin speakers. Both words meant a temporary sleeping place. Both words conveyed the Christian conviction that the dead in a graveyard are "asleep" awaiting their resurrection.

20. The English word *cemetery*, etymologically derived from the Latin *coemeterium*, is a theological concept. Thus, every time people use the word cemetery, knowingly or unknowingly, they echo the Christian conviction that a cemetery is a place where the dead are temporarily "asleep."

21. Cremation contradicts, even jettisons, numerous funeral hymns that speak about the deceased bodies sleeping in their graves, and thus many Christian hymns can no longer be logically sung at cremation funerals.

22. St. Paul in 1 Corinthians 15:44 says, by way of an analogy, that the deceased human body lying in a grave is like a planted seed in the soil, and on Resurrection Day it will rise

like a new plant, the latter being a spiritual (glorified) body. Cremation destroys this analogy, for a burned seed does not produce a new plant.

23. Today some Christians scatter the ashes of a cremated person, not realizing this practice was once done only with the ashes of cremated criminals in order to erase society's memory of their evil acts.

24. Crematory operators do not scour the inside of the furnace after each body is cremated. Thus, the survivors of a cremated body invariably receive a small amount of ashes from a previous body, and similarly, a small amount of their loved one's ashes are left behind that will become a part of the ashes of another cremated person.

25. Christians have always desired to be saved from the eternal flames of hell, a phenomenon noted by Jesus in Matthew 10:28. Thus, many ask: "How can it be theologically acceptable to have deceased bodies of Christians destroyed by hell-like fire in cremation?"

Facts Not Taught or Told about Embalmment

As noted in chapter 12, Christians in North America have for more than a century accepted embalming of the dead without any serious theological evaluation, primarily because they do not know and have not been told what embalming a dead body involves. The following facts are offered to help Christians understand this common mortuary custom.

1. There are only two cases of embalming (Jacob and Joseph) mentioned in the Bible, and neither has any biblical precedence or support. The Bible does not indicate that Christians are to imitate the embalming of Jacob and Joseph. Both embalming accounts are merely descriptive, not prescriptive.

2. Early in the life of the church, St. Antony (AD 251–356), founder of monasticism, directed Christians in Egypt not to embalm/mummify their deceased bodies. He said the practice was unbiblical and contrary to what had been done with the deceased bodies of the prophets and patriarchs and also with the crucified body of Jesus Christ.

3. Although embalming today is somewhat less macabre than it was in ancient Egypt, it still desecrates the human body. For its organs are punctured in order to siphon all the blood, liquids, and gases from it. These are considered waste material similar to other waste in society and flushed into the city's sewage system, all done in order to make the dead body look good for public viewing.

4. Embalming involves the use of highly toxic, carcinogenic chemicals. Hence, government regulations require embalmers to wear respirators and full-body coverings when they are engaged in embalming.

5. When the average human body is embalmed, about two gallons of formaldehyde (a.k.a. formalin) are injected into the body to complete the embalming process.

6. Embalming fluids pollute the soil after the body in the casket decays in the grave. In some instances it also pollutes the underground water supply.

7. Although not widely known by the public, embalming is not legally required in the United States and Canada. Hence, there is no need for Christians to choose embalmment.

8. Contrary to a widely held myth, sometimes spread by funeral directors, embalming does not make it safer hygienically for the public to view a deceased body at a funeral. Before the late 1800s, people viewed unembalmed bodies for centuries without any ill effects.

9. Reputable mortuaries honor requests not to embalm a deceased person's body. These mortuaries keep the body

refrigerated, and they also permit private viewing for relatives before burial.

10. Embalming serves primarily socio-psychological needs of the deceased person's surviving family and friends.

11. Research shows that embalming contributes to our culture's death-denial mentality.

12. There is no biblical support for embalming the dead.

13. The churches of Eastern Orthodoxy and Orthodox Jews do not approve of embalming for their deceased members.

Conclusion

Had Christian teachers, pastors, priests, and theologians made Christians in the past made aware of the above facts concerning cremation, they would likely not be contributing to the current, continuing rise of cremation rates, at least not to the same degree. All too often, well-meaning Christians, unknowingly influenced by their secular culture, do things out of ignorance. Many Christians who today favor cremation are an example of such ignorance. They have not been taught or told that Christians for centuries opposed and rejected cremating the dead; nor have been taught or told why they did so.

Similarly, they have not been taught or told the historical, biblical, and theological reasons why their Christian ancestors and their descendants did not embalm their departed loved ones. The lack of this information has not been beneficial for biblically minded Christians.

INDEX

Puckle, Bertram S., 147
Pueblo Indians, 24
Puticuli, 21, 111, 112
Pyre, Roman funeral, 45, 47
Pyre, funeral,condemned by
    Christians, 48

Queen Victoria, 6, 180
Queenan, Joe, 103

Rabbinic era, 41
Rebekah (Isaac's wife), 30
Reformed Church of America,
    130
Reformed Jews, 49
Resomation (defined), 66
Resomation Limited, 66, 67
Resurrection, doctrine of, x, xi,
    xxi, 8, 26, 42, 48, 56, 60, 79,
    82, 83, 84, 86, 90
Resurrection, post resurrection
    appearances of Christ, 17, 92,
    94, 119, 141
Resurrection Day, 141
Resurrection, doctrine of, passim
Rig Veda, 18
Roddenberry, Gene, 55
Roman Catholic bishops, 68
Roman Catholic Church, xx, 7,
    9, 10, 54, 56, 103, 126, 127,
    136, 142, 154
Romulus, 20
Rush, Alfred C., 74, 117
Russian Orthodox Cathedral of St.
    John the Baptist, 129
Russian Orthodox Church, 128
Rutherford, H. Richard, 76

St. Antony, 177, 178, 180, 187, 199
St. Augustine, 78, 79, 82, 150
St. Chrysostom, 78, 82
St. Cyprian, 117
St. Paul, passim
Same-sex marriage, 137
Samuel, O.T. prophet, 33
Santayana, George, 89
Sarah, Abraham's wife, 30
Sati (suttee), 21, 22
Saul, King, 33, 38, 39, 53
Schaaf, Philip, 85
Schalling, Martin, 104
Schleich, Carl Ludwig, 95
Schuller, Robert, 54
Scott-Moncrieff, Philip David, 179
Scripps Howard News Service, 91
Secularism, 150, 153
Senn, Frank, 160
Shaftsbury, Lord, 143
Shelley, Mary Wollstonecraft, 5
Shelley, Percy Bysche, 5
Shoemaker, Eugene, 56
Sikhs, 47
"Sleep," death as, 81, 82, 83, 93,
    109, 113
Social conformity, 12
Sodom and Gomorrah, 35, 101
Sophocles, Greek poet, 19
Southern Baptist Convention, 130,
    132
Spartans, 19
Spencer, A.J., 179, 180
Spiritualists, 49
Stark, Rodney, 152
Stephen, first Christian martyr, 74
Suicide, 18, 73, 75
Sulla, 20